The
'No Equipment Necessary'
Guide to Standout
Homemade Ice Cream

Easy No-Churn
ICE CREAM

HEATHER TEMPLETON
HEATHER'S HOME BAKERY

PAGE STREET
PUBLISHING CO.

Distributed by Macmillan, sales in Canada by The Canadian Manda Group.

26   25   24   23   22   1   2   3   4   5

ISBN-13: 978-1-64567-598-3
ISBN-10: 1-64567-598-X

Library of Congress Control Number: 2022930180

Cover and book design by Kylie Alexander for Page Street Publishing Co.
Photography by Heather Templeton

Printed and bound in the United States of America

Dedication

To my family, my friends and absolutely every single person
who has an incessant sweet tooth for ice cream,
this book is for you. I hope you love it.

Contents

INTRODUCTION

Welcome to *Easy No-Churn Ice Cream*! I am so happy that you're here, and together we are going to create mouthwatering frozen treats with absolutely no ice cream maker needed.

Spoiler: I used to own an ice cream maker. My husband and I got one for our wedding nearly 14 years ago, and to be completely honest, I might have used it twice. I ended up donating it during one of my seasonal house cleanings and I never regretted it. Years later, I began experimenting with no-churn ice cream. The amazing concoction of sweetened condensed milk creates an incredibly creamy and completely frozen ice cream treat. Gone are the days of soft serve as your only homemade option! Today, we bring real ice creams to the forefront of your dessert creations and trust me when I say, they will absolutely shine.

To make these treats, you need only a handful of ingredients and a little bit of patience. The freeze time is incredibly important to the finished product, ensuring that it is set before being enjoyed.

Now, this book contains fifty base recipes, all ranging from classic to utterly unique. But I take it a step further and add recommendations per page to help you "mix it up" even more! Take a glance at the variations included with each recipe and get ready to add even more fabulous flavors to your ice cream repertoire.

I am thrilled to walk through the no-churn ice cream making process with you and can't wait to get started. So, without further ado, let's dive right in.

XO,
Heather

Classics

Once deemed a "summertime treat" by many, ice cream has become a decadence that is enjoyed year round. The texture of no-churn ice cream is identical to its store-bought counterpart and the flavor is far superior. With only a handful of ingredients per recipe, you can gauge exactly what is going into your desserts. No ice cream maker is required, and only 5 to 10 minutes of preparation time per base ice cream recipe is needed. This allows you ample time to enjoy your treats, while being able to relax knowing exactly what is going into each and every one of them.

This chapter brings your favorite flavors to life in a whole new way. Enter: the classics. Creamy Vanilla (page 10), Rich Chocolate (page 13), Bold Coffee (page 17) and Nostalgic Cookies and Cream (page 18) are among many frozen childhood delights that you can easily recreate at home with a few simple, better-for-you ingredients while still tasting incredible. Healthier overall and just as delicious, these frozen desserts will keep you coming back for more every single time.

CREAMY VANILLA

This recipe yields roughly 12–14 standard scoops.

1 (14-oz [414-ml]) can sweetened condensed milk

1 tbsp (15 ml) pure vanilla extract

½ cup (120 ml) half-and-half

1½ cups (360 ml) heavy cream

There's arguably no more classic of a flavor than traditional vanilla. This ultra-creamy vanilla ice cream uses pure vanilla extract to create a strong and uninhibited vanilla flavor. Pure vanilla extract might be a bit more expensive than the artificial alternative, but I strongly recommend choosing it over the artificial counterpart. Using high-quality and real ingredients in this no-churn vanilla ice cream will yield an aromatic and bold flavor, rendering your base ice cream simply divine in both taste and scent.

In a medium-sized bowl, whisk together the sweetened condensed milk, pure vanilla extract and half-and-half, until the mixture is smooth. Set this aside. With a standing or hand mixer, whip the heavy cream until stiff peaks form, 60 to 90 seconds. Fold the sweetened condensed milk mixture into the cream that has been whipped. This is your ice cream base. You will want this to be as smooth as possible and lump free.

Pour the ice cream into an 8 x 8-inch (20 x 20-cm) baking pan (or a freezer-safe container of about the same size), and using your spatula, spread the ice cream evenly throughout the pan. Freeze the ice cream uncovered for 3 to 5 hours or overnight, until it is firm. Cover any leftovers with tinfoil or plastic wrap, and store them in the freezer for up to 3 weeks.

VARIATION: *Try adding in your favorite candy as a mix-in! A cup (170 g) of mix-ins would be more than enough, but hey, don't let me tell you how to enjoy your vanilla. A few berries would be wonderful as well.*

RICH CHOCOLATE

This recipe yields roughly 12–14 standard scoops.

Chocolate can easily be described as the love language of the human race. In a variety of forms, it is the most popular dessert around the entire globe. More than 3 million tons of cocoa beans are processed and consumed each year. Thankfully, you only need a fraction of that to make this decadent and smooth no-churn rich chocolate ice cream. I use pure Dutch-processed cocoa in this recipe, which is specially neutralized to reduce the bitter flavor of traditional cocoa, resulting in a wonderfully smooth finish. With only five ingredients, this rich chocolate ice cream flavor really shines through and is absolutely irresistible.

1 (14-oz [414-ml]) can sweetened condensed milk

1 tbsp (15 ml) pure vanilla extract

½ cup (120 ml) half-and-half

½ cup (50 g) Dutch-processed cocoa powder (unsweetened)

1½ cups (360 ml) heavy cream

In a medium-sized bowl, whisk together the sweetened condensed milk, pure vanilla extract and half-and-half, until the mixture is smooth. Stir in the cocoa powder until no loose powder remains. Set this aside. With a standing or hand mixer, whip the heavy cream until stiff peaks form, 60 to 90 seconds. Fold the sweetened condensed milk mixture into the cream that has been whipped. This is your ice cream base. You will want this to be as smooth as possible and lump free.

Pour the ice cream into an 8 x 8–inch (20 x 20–cm) baking pan (or a freezer-safe container of about the same size), and using your spatula, spread the ice cream evenly throughout the pan. Freeze the ice cream uncovered for 3 to 5 hours or overnight, until it is firm. Cover any leftovers with tinfoil or plastic wrap, and store them in the freezer for up to 3 weeks.

VARIATION: *Try half Creamy Vanilla (page 10) and half Rich Chocolate for a marbled ice cream like none other. Simply divide the vanilla batter into two bowls and gently mix ¼ cup (25 g) of Dutch-processed cocoa powder to one bowl. Alternate pouring vanilla then chocolate into your pan, and swirl with a butter knife.*

STRAWBERRY SWIRL

This recipe yields roughly 12–14 standard scoops.

For the Strawberry Swirl

30 medium-sized fresh strawberries (approximately 2 heaping cups [288 g])

½ cup (100 g) granulated sugar

2 tbsp (16 g) cornstarch

2 tbsp (30 ml) fresh squeezed lemon juice

For the Ice Cream

1 (14-oz [414-ml]) can sweetened condensed milk

1 tbsp (15 ml) pure vanilla extract

½ cup (120 ml) half-and-half

1½ cups (360 ml) heavy cream

VARIATION: *For a more traditionally smooth strawberry ice cream, purée the strawberry swirl mixture with 1 cup (240 ml) of the ice cream base. Gently mix the strawberry purée into the remainder of the base and freeze per the instructions. You can also add chopped fresh strawberries to either the recipe or the variation—it would be so refreshing.*

Strawberries are one of the most widely grown fruit crops in the entire world. It's no wonder this is true, as the strawberry is both sweet and tangy, with health benefits galore. Strawberries are said to aid in overall heart health, plus they are packed with vitamins and antioxidants.

This strawberry swirl ice cream uses fresh, ripe strawberries to pack the most strawberry flavor into a creamy vanilla ice cream base. And I don't skimp on the swirl—there is plenty of it to go around and around again.

To make the strawberry swirl, hull the strawberries by removing the green stems. Slice each strawberry in half. Place the berries, granulated sugar, cornstarch and fresh squeezed lemon juice in a medium-sized saucepan. Place the pan on the stovetop over medium-high heat. Using a potato masher, begin to mash the fruit and ingredients until they come together as it starts to warm up. After 1 to 2 minutes of cooking, the mixture will begin to bubble. Lower the heat to medium, and stir frequently until the fruit swirl thickens, another 1 to 2 minutes. Remove the mixture from the heat and transfer to a bowl. Refrigerate until completely cool, about 30 minutes.

In a medium-sized bowl, make the ice cream by whisking together the sweetened condensed milk, pure vanilla extract and half-and-half, until the mixture is smooth. Set this aside. With a standing or hand mixer, whip the heavy cream until stiff peaks form, 60 to 90 seconds. Fold the sweetened condensed milk mixture into the cream that has been whipped. This is your ice cream base. You will want this to be as smooth as possible and lump free.

Remove the strawberry swirl mixture from the refrigerator. Drop the mixture by full tablespoons (15 ml) all over the top of the ice cream base, using all of it up. Take a butter knife or fork, and swirl the mixture into the base, ensuring that it is dispersed throughout the ice cream.

Pour the ice cream into an 8 x 8-inch (20 x 20-cm) baking pan (or a freezer-safe container of about the same size), and using your spatula, spread the ice cream evenly throughout the pan. Freeze the ice cream uncovered for 3 to 5 hours or overnight, until it is firm. Cover any leftovers with tinfoil or plastic wrap, and store them in the freezer for up to 3 weeks.

BOLD COFFEE

This recipe yields roughly 12–14 standard scoops.

I love coffee. Consuming this glorious beverage is definitely a highlight of each day, and when I wanted to create a wonderfully balanced coffee-flavored frozen treat, pure coffee extract was the ultimate way to go. Concentrated to pack in as much coffee flavor as possible, this recipe uses a high-quality extract for maximum flavor and a creamy consistency throughout the batch.

1 (14-oz [414-ml]) can sweetened condensed milk

1 tbsp (15 ml) pure vanilla extract

1 tbsp (15 ml) pure coffee extract

½ cup (120 ml) half-and-half

1½ cups (360 ml) heavy cream

In a medium-sized bowl, whisk together the sweetened condensed milk, pure vanilla extract, pure coffee extract and half-and-half, until the mixture is smooth. Set this aside. With a standing or hand mixer, whip the heavy cream until stiff peaks form, 60 to 90 seconds. Fold the sweetened condensed milk mixture into the cream that has been whipped. This is your ice cream base. You will want this to be as smooth as possible and lump free.

Pour the ice cream into an 8 x 8-inch (20 x 20-cm) baking pan (or a freezer-safe container of about the same size), and using your spatula, spread the ice cream evenly throughout the pan. Freeze the ice cream uncovered for 3 to 5 hours or overnight, until it is firm. Cover any leftovers with tinfoil or plastic wrap and store them in the freezer for up to 3 weeks.

VARIATION: *Try swirling in some homemade caramel (page 75) and even mixing in some of your favorite chocolate chips to bring a latte flair to this classic.*

NOSTALGIC COOKIES AND CREAM

This recipe yields roughly 12–14 standard scoops.

1 (14-oz [414-ml]) can sweetened condensed milk

2 tsp (10 ml) pure vanilla extract

½ cup (120 ml) half-and-half

1½ cups (360 ml) heavy cream

15 chocolate sandwich cookies

We've chatted about both vanilla and chocolate thus far, so we've come to the point in this book where they come together in harmonious unity. Growing up, cookies and cream was my all-time favorite ice cream flavor. It was hard to imagine loving another ice cream more than the tantalizing combination of creamy vanilla ice cream and chopped chocolate sandwich cookies.

I use Oreos® in this recipe, but you can pick your favorite chocolate sandwich cookie and sub it right in. This simple and nostalgic recipe will surely become a family favorite for years to come.

In a medium-sized bowl, whisk together the sweetened condensed milk, pure vanilla extract and half-and-half, until the mixture is smooth. Set this aside. With a standing or hand mixer, whip the heavy cream until stiff peaks form, 60 to 90 seconds. Fold the sweetened condensed milk mixture into the cream that has been whipped. This is your ice cream base. You will want this to be as smooth as possible and lump free.

Place the sandwich cookies in a large sturdy plastic bag and seal it, ensuring most of the air has been removed first. Using a rolling pin, roll over the cookies to break them up into larger chunks. Alternatively, you can crush them by hand, breaking each cookie roughly into fourths. If you prefer smaller chunks, simply crush the cookies further. If you prefer larger chunks, crush them less. Place the crushed cookies into the ice cream mixture and gently mix, ensuring that the cookies are well distributed within the batch of ice cream.

Pour the ice cream into an 8 x 8–inch (20 x 20–cm) baking pan (or a freezer-safe container of about the same size), and using your spatula, spread the ice cream evenly throughout the pan. Freeze the ice cream uncovered for 3 to 5 hours or overnight, until it is firm. Cover any leftovers with tinfoil or plastic wrap, and store them in the freezer for up to 3 weeks.

VARIATION: *Try making the Rich Chocolate (page 13) and adding the crushed chocolate sandwich cookies to it.*

REFRESHING MINT CHOCOLATE CHIP

This recipe yields roughly 12–14 standard scoops.

Arguably one of the most popular ice cream flavors in the world, mint chocolate chip has seen its fair share of variations. Many of us remember the bright green ice cream from our youth. It was cool, refreshing and oh-so-minty. The cold chocolate chips were the finishing touches on a truly satisfying frozen treat.

My version of mint chocolate chip is not only no-churn and easy to whip up, but it requires no fake green food coloring or additives of any kind. Pure peppermint extract marries with semi-sweet chocolate chips in this modern, better-for-you reimagined classic.

1 (14-oz [414-ml]) can sweetened condensed milk

2 tsp (10 ml) pure vanilla extract

1 tsp pure peppermint extract

½ cup (120 ml) half-and-half

1½ cups (360 ml) heavy cream

1½ cups (248 g) semi-sweet chocolate chips

In a medium-sized bowl, whisk together the sweetened condensed milk, pure vanilla extract, pure peppermint extract and half-and-half, until the mixture is smooth. Set this aside. With a standing or hand mixer, whip the heavy cream until stiff peaks form, 60 to 90 seconds. Fold the sweetened condensed milk mixture into the cream that has been whipped. This is your ice cream base. You will want this to be as smooth as possible and lump free. Add the semi-sweet chocolate chips to the bowl and stir them in, ensuring that they are evenly distributed throughout the ice cream base.

Pour the ice cream into an 8 x 8-inch (20 x 20-cm) baking pan (or a freezer-safe container of about the same size), and using your spatula, spread the ice cream evenly throughout the pan. Freeze the ice cream uncovered for 3 to 5 hours or overnight, until it is firm. Cover any leftovers with tinfoil or plastic wrap, and store them in the freezer for up to 3 weeks.

VARIATION: Prefer dark chocolate? Sub in dark chocolate chips or even milk chocolate if that's your jam! Mini chips would be a fun twist too, especially for an ice cream sandwich using mint chocolate shortbread (page 135).

LOADED PEANUT BUTTER CUP

This recipe yields roughly 12–14 standard scoops.

1 (14-oz [414-ml]) can sweetened condensed milk

2 tsp (10 ml) pure vanilla extract

⅓ cup (86 g) all-natural, no-sugar-added creamy peanut butter

½ cup (120 ml) half-and-half

1½ cups (360 ml) heavy cream

30 mini peanut butter cups

VARIATION: *Add a fudge swirl to up the decadence-ante on this one. Simply swirl in a ½ cup (168 g) of your favorite store-bought fudge before freezing as instructed.*

Peanut butter plus chocolate is a match made in culinary paradise. The combination first became popular in the late 1920s. From there, the world's obsession began to grow and today we have hundreds of mouthwatering peanut butter and chocolate recipes to choose from.

This loaded peanut butter cup ice cream begins with a perfectly creamy peanut butter ice cream base. Loads of crushed peanut butter cups are added to the base, rendering it quite possibly a peanut butter lover's dream come true.

I chose Adams® creamy peanut butter (no sugar added—this is simply crushed peanuts and salt) plus mini Reese's® peanut butter cups for this recipe, but you can add in your favorite brands to create this glorious peanut butter plus chocolate flavor.

In a medium-sized bowl, whisk together the sweetened condensed milk, pure vanilla extract, peanut butter and half-and-half, until the mixture is smooth. Set this aside. With a standing or hand mixer, whip the heavy cream until stiff peaks form, 60 to 90 seconds. Fold the sweetened condensed milk mixture into the cream that has been whipped. This is your ice cream base. You will want this to be as smooth as possible and lump free.

Unwrap the mini peanut butter cups. Place them in a large plastic bag and seal it. Gently roll a rolling pin over the peanut butter cups to crush them into chunks, being careful as they are a softer candy. Alternatively, you can crush them by hand, roughly breaking them into four pieces per cup. For larger chunks of peanut butter cups, simply crush them less. For smaller chunks of peanut butter cups, crush them more. Place the crushed peanut butter cups into the ice cream base and stir to combine, ensuring that there is an even distribution of cups throughout the ice cream batter.

Pour the ice cream into an 8 x 8-inch (20 x 20-cm) baking pan (or a freezer-safe container of about the same size), and using your spatula, spread the ice cream evenly throughout the pan. Freeze the ice cream uncovered for 3 to 5 hours or overnight, until it is firm. Cover any leftovers with tinfoil or plastic wrap, and store them in the freezer for up to 3 weeks.

Fruit + Tea

An array of sweet, seasonal fruits are blended into many of this chapter's no-churn ice cream flavors. I also brew some aromatic tea for an elegant frozen take on warming beverages. From fan favorites like raspberries and bananas, to less traditional flavors like Frozen London Fog (page 36) and Huckleberry Swirl (page 33), there's something for nearly everyone in this harvest of fruit and herbal flavors.

When choosing fruits for these recipes, fresh is always best. Many fresh fruits retain more nutrients over their frozen alternatives. Nutrients in fruit are at their highest right after being picked. Organic berries are preferable, as are any local fruits and teas you can locate. Ensure that your fruits are ripe and sweet, as this aids in the overall top quality and flavor of each recipe.

RASPBERRY WHITE CHOCOLATE CHIP

This recipe yields roughly 12–14 standard scoops.

For the Raspberry Sauce

2 cups (246 g) fresh raspberries

½ cup (100 g) granulated sugar

2 tbsp (16 g) cornstarch

2 tbsp (30 ml) fresh squeezed lemon juice

For the Ice Cream

1 (14-oz [414-ml]) can sweetened condensed milk

1 tbsp (15 ml) pure vanilla extract

½ cup (120 ml) half-and-half

1½ cups (360 ml) heavy cream

2 cups (330 g) white chocolate chips

VARIATION: *Use your favorite berry in place of raspberries! Black-berries, blueberries or strawberries would all work in this recipe as a one-to-one fruit substitute.*

A tantalizing combination of fresh raspberry sauce and sweet white chocolate chips create a truly spectacular no-churn ice cream to begin this chapter. The rich and creamy vanilla base is loaded with ripe berries that are cooked down into a perfectly sweet and perfectly tart sauce, and this is married with smooth white chocolate. The result is an ultra-satisfying treat that is sweet and packed with fruit flavor.

To make the raspberry sauce, place the raspberries, granulated sugar, cornstarch and fresh squeezed lemon juice in a medium-sized saucepan. Place the pan on the stovetop over medium-high heat. Using a potato masher, begin to mash the fruit and ingredients until they come together as the mixture starts to warm up. After 1 to 2 minutes of cooking, the mixture will begin to bubble. Lower the heat to medium and stir frequently until the fruit sauce thickens, another 1 to 2 minutes. Remove the mixture from the heat, and transfer to a bowl. Refrigerate until completely cool, for about 30 minutes.

In a medium-sized bowl, make the ice cream by whisking together the sweetened condensed milk, pure vanilla extract and half-and-half, until the mixture is smooth. Set this aside. With a standing or hand mixer, whip the heavy cream until stiff peaks form, 60 to 90 seconds. Fold the sweetened condensed milk mixture into the cream that has been whipped. This is your ice cream base. You will want this to be as smooth as possible and lump free. Pour the white chocolate chips into the base and mix to combine.

Remove the raspberry sauce mixture from the refrigerator. Drop the mixture by full tablespoons (15 ml) all over the top of the ice cream base, using all of it up. Take a butter knife or fork and swirl the mixture into the base, ensuring that it is dispersed throughout the ice cream.

Pour the ice cream into an 8 x 8–inch (20 x 20-cm) baking pan (or a freezer-safe container of about the same size), and using your spatula, spread the ice cream evenly throughout the pan. Freeze the ice cream uncovered for 3 to 5 hours or overnight, until it is firm. Cover any leftovers with tinfoil or plastic wrap, and store them in the freezer for up to 3 weeks.

LEMON CURD RIPPLE

This recipe yields roughly 12–14 standard scoops.

Lemon is my all-time favorite citrus. It is so tart and flavorful. When it is mixed with butter and egg yolks to create a classic lemon curd, it's downright irresistible. This lemon curd is swirled into creamy lemon ice cream, making it quite possibly the most perfect lemony ice cream out there.

To make the lemon curd, begin by beating the egg yolks, granulated sugar and fresh squeezed lemon juice together in a small bowl until combined. Cut the butter into four chunks and set them aside.

Pour the egg yolk mixture into a medium saucepan and cook it over low heat. After about 5 minutes, gently add the chunks of butter and continue to stir until they have melted and the curd has thickened slightly, about another 7 minutes. You will want to whisk the curd constantly so that the eggs do not "cook." Remove the curd from heat and immediately strain. This will remove any small parts of the egg that might have cooked. Add the heavy cream to the warm curd, and whisk until it is completely incorporated, for about 10 seconds. Pour the curd into a medium-sized bowl and cover it with a layer of plastic wrap. You will want the plastic to touch the top of the curd, so as it cools, it does not form a "skin" on top. Place the curd in the refrigerator to cool completely.

In a medium-sized bowl, make the ice cream by whisking together the sweetened condensed milk, pure vanilla extract, pure lemon extract and half-and-half, until the mixture is smooth. Set this aside. With a standing or hand mixer, whip the heavy cream until stiff peaks form, 60 to 90 seconds. Fold the sweetened condensed milk mixture into the cream that has been whipped. This is your ice cream base. You will want this to be as smooth as possible and lump free. Pour this into an 8 x 8-inch (20 x 20-cm) baking dish .

Remove the lemon curd from the refrigerator. Drop large tablespoons (15 ml) of the curd over the top of the ice cream base, using all of it up. Take a butter knife or fork and swirl the curd into the base, ensuring that it is well dispersed throughout the ice cream.

Freeze the ice cream uncovered for 3 to 5 hours or overnight, until it is firm. Cover any leftovers with tinfoil or plastic wrap, and store them in the freezer for up to 3 weeks.

For the Lemon Curd

6 large egg yolks

¾ cup (150 g) granulated sugar

½ cup (120 ml) fresh squeezed lemon juice

½ cup (114 g) salted butter, softened

2 tbsp (30 ml) heavy cream

For the Ice Cream

1 (14-oz [414-ml]) can sweetened condensed milk

2 tsp (10 ml) pure vanilla extract

1 tbsp (15 ml) pure lemon extract

½ cup (120 ml) half-and-half

1½ cups (360 ml) heavy cream

VARIATION: *For extra lemony goodness, add an extra 1 tablespoon (15 ml) of pure lemon extract to the ice cream base before swirling in the lemon curd. Continue making the recipe as instructed.*

BANANA SPLIT

This recipe yields roughly 12–14 standard scoops.

1 (14-oz [414-ml]) can sweetened condensed milk

2 tsp (10 ml) pure vanilla extract

½ cup (120 ml) half-and-half

1½ cups (360 ml) heavy cream

½ cup (75 g) sliced bananas

2 tsp (10 ml) strawberry emulsion

3–4 drops of all-natural red food coloring (optional)

¼ cup (25 g) Dutch-processed cocoa powder (unsweetened)

The classic banana split was born in 1904. Now the gloriously fruity + fudgy + nutty original is a layered mix of many sweet elements that come together harmoniously in one bowl. This no-churn version takes those same elements and simplifies them into one pan of ice cream. You get all the glorious banana split flavor in one (or two or more) convenient scoop(s).

In a medium-sized bowl, whisk together the sweetened condensed milk, pure vanilla extract and half-and-half, until the mixture is smooth. Set this aside. With a standing or hand mixer, whip the heavy cream until stiff peaks form, 60 to 90 seconds. Fold the sweetened condensed milk mixture into the cream that has been whipped. This is your ice cream base. You will want this to be as smooth as possible and lump free.

Divide the ice cream base into three medium bowls.

Mash or purée the bananas until only small chunks remain and add this mixture to the first bowl. Gently fold this together until it is well incorporated, about 30 seconds.

Into bowl number two, add the strawberry emulsion and the red food coloring, if you choose to use it. The food coloring will not affect the flavor of the ice cream, only the color. Mix until fully incorporated, about 30 seconds. Place this bowl into the refrigerator.

Into bowl number three, add the cocoa powder. Gently stir until you see no unmixed cocoa powder remaining in the bowl. Place this bowl into the refrigerator.

(continued)

BANANA SPLIT (cont.)

½ cup (168 g) chocolate fudge, divided

½ cup (73 g) salted peanuts, chopped

Whipped cream for topping (optional)

Maraschino cherries for topping (optional)

Pour the banana ice cream into an 8 x 8–inch (20 x 20–cm) baking pan (or a freezer-safe container of about the same size), and using your spatula, spread the ice cream evenly throughout the pan. Freeze the ice cream for 20 to 30 minutes, or until it is slightly set and no longer liquid. Remove the pan from the freezer, and drizzle ¼ cup (84 g) of the fudge evenly over the top. Pour the strawberry ice cream over the fudge-topped banana layer. Place the pan back into the freezer for another 20 to 30 minutes, or until the strawberry layer is also no longer liquid. Finally, remove the pan from the freezer and drizzle the remaining ¼ cup (84 g) of fudge evenly over the strawberry layer. Pour the chocolate ice cream over the fudge-topped strawberry ice cream. Sprinkle the chopped peanuts on top. Freeze uncovered for 3 to 5 hours or overnight, until it is firm. Serve topped with whipped cream and a maraschino cherry, if desired.

Cover any leftovers with tinfoil or plastic wrap and store them in the freezer for up to 3 weeks.

VARIATION: *If you prefer to use real strawberries instead of strawberry emulsion, simply make one-third of the strawberry swirl mix-in (page 14) and utilize the variation to purée the fruit for a creamy strawberry ice cream.*

HUCKLEBERRY SWIRL

This recipe yields roughly 12–14 standard scoops.

Huckleberries are native to the Pacific Northwest and thrive in the mountainous terrain. These little berries are often confused with blueberries but have their own distinct flavor that is slightly more tart than a standard blueberry.

This Huckleberry Swirl ice cream uses fresh huckleberries to create a homemade jam-like swirl. If you live in an area where it is hard to get fresh huckleberries, you can absolutely use store-bought huckleberry jam. Choose a brand with a brief list of all-natural ingredients, as this will be closest to my homemade version.

To make the huckleberry sauce, place the huckleberries, granulated sugar, cornstarch and fresh lemon juice in a medium-sized sauce-pan. Place the pan on the stovetop over medium-high heat. Using a potato masher, begin to mash the fruit and ingredients until they come together as it starts to warm up. After 1 to 2 minutes of cooking, the mixture will begin to bubble. Lower the heat to medium, and stir frequently until the fruit sauce thickens, another 1 to 2 minutes. Remove the mixture from the heat and transfer to a bowl. Refrigerate the mixture until completely cool, about 30 minutes.

In a medium-sized bowl, make the ice cream by whisking together the sweetened condensed milk, pure vanilla extract and half-and-half, until the mixture is smooth. Set this aside. With a standing or hand mixer, whip the heavy cream until stiff peaks form, 60 to 90 seconds. Fold the sweetened condensed milk mixture into the cream that has been whipped. This is your ice cream base. You will want this to be as smooth as possible, and lump free.

If you are using the store-bought jam alternative, follow the same instructions on how to swirl it into your ice cream base.

For the Huckleberry Sauce

2 cups (246 g) fresh huckleberries*

½ cup (100 g) granulated sugar

2 tbsp (16 g) cornstarch

2 tbsp (30 ml) fresh squeezed lemon juice

*If you cannot find fresh huckleberries, you may substitute ¾ cup (180 ml) of store-bought huckleberry jam for the huckleberry sauce.

For the Ice Cream

1 (14-oz [414-ml]) can sweetened condensed milk

1 tbsp (15 ml) pure vanilla extract

½ cup (120 ml) half-and-half

1½ cups (360 ml) heavy cream

HUCKLEBERRY SWIRL (cont.)

Remove the huckleberry sauce mixture from the refrigerator. Drop the mixture by full tablespoons (15 ml) all over the top of the ice cream base, using all of it up. Take a butter knife or fork, and swirl the mixture into the base, ensuring that it is dispersed throughout the ice cream.

Pour the ice cream into an 8 x 8-inch (20 x 20-cm) baking pan (or a freezer-safe container of about the same size), and using your spatula, spread the ice cream evenly throughout the pan. Freeze the ice cream uncovered for 3 to 5 hours or overnight, until it is firm. Cover any leftovers with tinfoil or plastic wrap, and store them in the freezer for up to 3 weeks.

VARIATION: *Love whole huckleberries? Use the fruit whole if you prefer to keep it simple! Or add fruit as a mix-in with the huckleberry sauce for a good bit more huckleberry flavor.*

FROZEN LONDON FOG

This recipe yields roughly 12–14 standard scoops.

½ cup (120 ml) half-and-half

4 Earl Grey teabags

1 (14-oz [414-ml]) can sweetened condensed milk

1 tbsp (15 ml) pure vanilla extract

1½ cups (360 ml) heavy cream

The London Fog became a tea drink sensation in Canada in the 1990s. With its Earl Grey base, steamed whole milk and sweet vanilla syrup, it was the "tea latte" equivalent to its espresso-based counterpart.

This frozen London Fog takes the bold and poignant flavor of Earl Grey tea and steeps it in half-and-half before chilling the mixture to then blend with cream and vanilla. It's a perfect tea lover's delight, and I'm betting that even a tea skeptic would nod their head in approval.

Place the half-and-half in a microwave-proof glass or mug, and heat it for 45 to 60 seconds on high (or until hot). Be cautious when removing the glass or mug, as the cream can bubble up. Steep the four teabags in the warm cream for 10 minutes, ensuring that the bags are fully immersed in the cream. Gently remove the teabags and squeeze out any excess cream into the glass, because you will want every bit of this Earl Grey–infused goodness. Place the tea-infused cream into the refrigerator until it is cool, for about 30 minutes.

In a medium-sized bowl, whisk together the sweetened condensed milk, pure vanilla extract and Earl Grey–infused half-and-half, until the mixture is smooth. Set this aside. With a standing or hand mixer, whip the heavy cream until stiff peaks form, 60 to 90 seconds. Fold the sweetened condensed milk mixture into the cream that has been whipped. This is your ice cream base. You will want this to be as smooth as possible and lump free.

Pour the ice cream into an 8 x 8-inch (20 x 20–cm) baking pan (or a freezer-safe container of about the same size), and using your spatula, spread the ice cream evenly throughout the pan. Freeze the ice cream uncovered for 3 to 5 hours or overnight, until it is firm. Cover any leftovers with tinfoil or plastic wrap, and store them in the freezer for up to 3 weeks.

VARIATION: *Omit the vanilla extract for a more traditionally simple Earl Grey ice cream.*

LEMON LAVENDER

This recipe yields roughly 12–14 standard scoops.

Lemon and lavender is a fruity, floral flavor combination that mimics the very essence of spring. A powerful herb used for everything from cuts and scrapes to insomnia, lavender is best known for its mild sweet taste and scent that can be enjoyed in a wide variety of edibles.

Organic lavender extract paste yields its beautiful flavor to this creamy lemon no-churn ice cream. I've measured out enough for a moderate ratio of lavender to lemon, but if you love a more powerful lavender flavor, by all means increase the amount to your liking.

1 (14-oz [414-ml]) can sweetened condensed milk

2 tsp (10 ml) pure vanilla extract

1 tsp lavender extract paste

1 tbsp (15 ml) pure lemon extract

½ cup (120 ml) half-and-half

1½ cups (360 ml) heavy cream

In a medium-sized bowl, whisk together the sweetened condensed milk, pure vanilla extract, lavender extract paste, pure lemon extract and half-and-half, until the mixture is smooth. Set this aside. With a standing or hand mixer, whip the heavy cream until stiff peaks form, 60 to 90 seconds. Fold the sweetened condensed milk mixture into the cream that has been whipped. This is your ice cream base. You will want this to be as smooth as possible and lump free.

Pour the ice cream into an 8 x 8-inch (20 x 20-cm) baking pan (or a freezer-safe container of about the same size), and using your spatula, spread the ice cream evenly throughout the pan. Freeze the ice cream uncovered for 3 to 5 hours or overnight, until it is firm. Cover any leftovers with tinfoil or plastic wrap, and store them in the freezer for up to 3 weeks.

VARIATION: *For extra lemony goodness, swirl in the lemon curd from the recipe on page 29.*

CREAMY MANGO

This recipe yields roughly 12–14 standard scoops.

2 cups (330 g) sliced fresh mango (about 2 medium-sized mangos)

1 (14-oz [414-ml]) can sweetened condensed milk

1 tbsp (15 ml) pure vanilla extract

½ cup (120 ml) half-and-half

1½ cups (360 ml) heavy cream

The mango has been touted as a sacred fruit. Originating over four millennia ago, this tropical fruit is wonderful in desserts and savory dishes alike. Its sweet and smooth flavor is intoxicating on its own and added to homemade no-churn ice cream, it becomes a satisfying staple for any mango lover.

In this recipe, I cream fresh mango and fold it into classic vanilla ice cream. The result is pure mango goodness shining though this ultra-easy frozen goodie.

Place the mango slices in a blender and purée, or mash by hand until only small chunks remain.

In a medium-sized bowl, whisk together the sweetened condensed milk, pure vanilla extract and half-and-half, until the mixture is smooth. Mix in the mango purée and set this aside. With a standing or hand mixer, whip the heavy cream until stiff peaks form, 60 to 90 seconds. Fold the sweetened condensed milk and mango mixture into the cream that has been whipped. This is your ice cream base. You will want this to be as smooth as possible and lump free.

Pour the ice cream into an 8 x 8-inch (20 x 20-cm) baking pan (or a freezer-safe container of about the same size), and using your spatula, spread the ice cream evenly throughout the pan. Freeze the ice cream uncovered for 3 to 5 hours or overnight, until it is firm. Cover any leftovers with tinfoil or plastic wrap, and store them in the freezer for up to 3 weeks.

VARIATION: *Adding chopped in-season mango to the base before freezing would give some texture to this creamy ice cream and double the mango flavor.*

SPICED AUTUMN PEAR

This recipe yields roughly 12–14 standard scoops.

We grow spectacular pears here in the great Pacific Northwest. They are soft yet crunchy, full of flavor and wonderfully sweet. We have acres and acres of pear orchards that bloom in late summer. Bartlett, Comice and D'Anjou are the most commonly harvested varieties in my native southern Oregon. You can use pretty much any variety of pear that you can find locally in this recipe, but I recommend D'Anjou because it is my favorite pear and the sweetest of the lot.

With its perfect balance of softened pears and an array of fall spices, this spiced autumn ice cream is sure to be an October staple for years to come.

Fill a medium saucepan with water to the halfway mark and add the pears. Place on the stovetop over high heat until it comes to a boil. Reduce the heat to medium-high and boil for 10 minutes. Remove the pan from the stove and strain the pears. Place them in a bowl and refrigerate until they are cool, for about 30 minutes. Remove the chilled pears and purée the mixture until it is smooth with only small chunks remaining.

In a medium-sized bowl, make the ice cream by whisking together the sweetened condensed milk, pure vanilla extract, cinnamon, nutmeg, cloves and half-and-half, until the mixture is smooth. Set this aside. With a standing or hand mixer, whip the heavy cream until stiff peaks form, 60 to 90 seconds. Fold the sweetened condensed milk mixture into the cream that has been whipped. This is your ice cream base. You will want this to be as smooth as possible and lump free.

Fold the puréed pears into the ice cream base, ensuring that pears are well distributed throughout the ice cream.

Pour the ice cream into an 8 x 8-inch (20 x 20–cm) baking pan (or a freezer-safe container of about the same size), and using your spatula, spread the ice cream evenly throughout the pan. Freeze the ice cream uncovered for 3 to 5 hours or overnight, until it is firm. Cover any leftovers with tinfoil or plastic wrap, and store them in the freezer for up to 3 weeks.

2 cups (250 g) cubed fresh pears (4–5 medium-sized pears)

1 (14-oz [414-ml]) can sweetened condensed milk

2 tsp (10 ml) pure vanilla extract

1 tsp ground cinnamon

½ tsp ground nutmeg

¼ tsp ground cloves

½ cup (120 ml) half-and-half

1½ cups (360 ml) heavy cream

VARIATION: *A fan of pears but not the spices? Simply omit them!*

On the Decadent Side

When we think ice cream, we automatically think decadent! But this chapter is extra special. In this section, I combine some of the sweetest, most heavenly pairings you will see in this book, from loads of sprinkles in my Sprinkle Birthday Cake Batter (page 46), all the way to Irish Cream Fudge (page 59), which boasts an actual fudge recipe blended right into the Irish cream–flavored ice cream base.

I derive many of my flavors from extracts, as they pack a flavor punch and eliminate the need for actual alcohol in some of these recipes—hello Creamy Kahlua (page 60), made with only Kahlua flavoring . . . we see you and we love you. I also LOAD up the mix-ins. There are no small brownie pieces in my Chocolate Brownie Chunk (page 51)—we make an entire small batch of brownies and use up EVERY SINGLE PIECE (you know, except for that bite or two you snuck while they were cooling . . . yeah, I saw you).

Enjoy all the flavor packed into the decadent side of no-churn ice cream.

SPRINKLE BIRTHDAY CAKE BATTER

This recipe yields roughly 12–14 standard scoops.

1 (14-oz [414-ml]) can sweetened condensed milk

2 tsp (10 ml) pure vanilla extract

1 tbsp (15 ml) cake batter flavoring

½ cup (120 ml) half-and-half

1½ cups (360 ml) heavy cream

½ cup (96 g) rainbow sprinkles

Cake batter is a supreme indulgence that carries a stigma due to the notion that raw egg consumption can be harmful. I've taken all the risk out of the batter by using high-quality cake batter flavoring for my decadent vanilla ice cream. Rainbow sprinkles complete this treat because sprinkles simply improve every single dessert that they rain down upon.

In a medium-sized bowl, whisk together the sweetened condensed milk, pure vanilla extract, cake batter flavoring and half-and-half, until the mixture is smooth. Set this aside. With a standing or hand mixer, whip the heavy cream until stiff peaks form, 60 to 90 seconds. Fold the sweetened condensed milk mixture into the cream that has been whipped. This is your ice cream base. You will want this to be as smooth as possible and lump free.

Pour the ice cream into an 8 x 8-inch (20 x 20-cm) baking pan (or a freezer-safe container of about the same size), and using your spatula, spread the ice cream evenly throughout the pan. Freeze the ice cream for about 20 minutes. You will want the ice cream to be slightly sturdier than liquid form so it can hold the sprinkles and they don't all sink to the bottom. Fold in the sprinkles, making sure that they are evenly distributed throughout the ice cream. Continue freezing uncovered for 3 to 5 hours or overnight, until it is firm. Cover any leftovers with tinfoil or plastic wrap, and store them in the freezer for up to 3 weeks.

VARIATION: *How about chocolate birthday cake batter? Yeah, I had to go there. Simply use the Rich Chocolate base recipe (page 13) and continue with this recipe for additions of the cake batter flavor and sprinkles . . . add in some chocolate sprinkles too, because really, why not?*

CHOCOLATE PEANUT BUTTER RIPPLE

This recipe yields roughly 12–14 standard scoops.

I revisit our fabulous peanut butter and chocolate combination in this chapter, only this time, I have a chocolate ice cream base with a homemade peanut butter ripple running through it. This peanut butter ripple is pure decadence. Using only a handful of simple ingredients, it lends its true peanut butter flavor effortlessly to the rich chocolate ice cream.

Dutch-processed cocoa powder is used in this recipe, which is my classic chocolate base. Dutch cocoa powder has been treated with an alkalizing agent. This takes the acidity down, rendering it less bitter than its untreated counterpart. All that is left is the deep, rich chocolate flavor—a perfect canvas for the peanut butter ripple to make its mark.

In a small bowl, make the peanut butter ripple by combining the peanut butter, melted butter, powdered sugar and pure vanilla extract. Whisk this mixture until it is fully incorporated, 10 to 15 seconds. Place the peanut butter ripple in the refrigerator to cool slightly. You do not want it to harden up before adding it to the ice cream base, so keep an eye on it—5 to 10 minutes is all it takes to thicken up. Pull the mixture out of the refrigerator and set it aside.

In a medium-sized bowl, make the ice cream by whisking together the sweetened condensed milk, pure vanilla extract and half-and-half, until the mixture is smooth. Stir in the cocoa powder until no loose powder remains. Set this aside. With a standing or hand mixer, whip the heavy cream until stiff peaks form, 60 to 90 seconds. Fold the sweetened condensed milk mixture into the cream that has been whipped. This is your ice cream base. You will want this to be as smooth as possible and lump free.

(continued)

For the Peanut Butter Ripple

1 cup (258 g) all-natural, no-sugar-added peanut butter (I used Adams salted creamy peanut butter)

⅓ cup (86 g) salted butter, melted

¼ cup (30 g) powdered sugar

¼ tsp pure vanilla extract

For the Ice Cream

1 (14-oz [414-ml]) can sweetened condensed milk

2 tsp (10 ml) pure vanilla extract

½ cup (120 ml) half-and-half

½ cup (50 g) Dutch-processed cocoa powder (unsweetened)

1½ cups (360 ml) heavy cream

CHOCOLATE PEANUT BUTTER RIPPLE (cont.)

Pour about a half of the chocolate ice cream base into an 8 x 8–inch (20 x 20–cm) baking pan (or a freezer-safe container of about the same size), and using your spatula, spread the ice cream evenly throughout the pan. Drizzle about half of the peanut butter ripple over the chocolate ice cream. Add the remainder of the chocolate ice cream base, and finally drizzle the remainder of the peanut butter ripple. With a butter knife or fork, swirl the mixture together to ensure it is evenly distributed throughout the ice cream. You can leave larger "pockets" of the ripple for larger chunks in your ice cream if you'd like—this is how I love to make it. Freeze the ice cream uncovered for 3 to 5 hours or overnight, until it is firm. Cover any leftovers with tinfoil or plastic wrap, and store them in the freezer for up to 3 weeks.

VARIATION: *For an explosion of peanut butter flavor, add a ½ cup (129 g) of creamy peanut butter to the base recipe, and then add 1 cup (250 g) of crushed peanut butter cups along with the peanut butter ripple. You can also make this recipe with the Creamy Vanilla base on page 10.*

CHOCOLATE BROWNIE CHUNK

This recipe yields roughly 12–14 standard scoops.

If you love chocolate ice cream and rich chocolate brownies, I've just married the two into one perfect chocolate-laden frozen treat. This recipe uses my rich chocolate ice cream base and includes a small batch of homemade double-chocolate brownies for that perfectly dense and satisfying dessert. Also, if you feel so led, you could double the brownie recipe, add half to the ice cream as the recipe calls for and serve the ice cream OVER the other half. Really, it's like chocolate goodness couldn't possibly get any better.

For the Small-Batch Brownies

6 tbsp (84 g) salted butter, melted

6 tbsp (37 g) Dutch-processed cocoa powder (unsweetened)

½ cup (100 g) granulated sugar

1 large egg

1 tsp pure vanilla extract

6 tbsp (48 g) all-purpose flour

⅓ cup (55 g) semi-sweet chocolate chips

Pinch of salt

To make the small-batch brownies, begin by spraying or lining a 6-inch (15-cm) round cake pan with parchment paper. Set this aside. Preheat the oven to 350°F (177°C).

Combine the melted butter and cocoa powder in a medium-sized bowl. With a standing mixer or by hand, mix until they are fully incorporated, about 15 seconds. Add the sugar and mix well. Add the egg and pure vanilla extract, mixing again until smooth. Add the flour and mix the batter until it is fully combined. Fold in the chocolate chips and add a pinch of salt. Pour the batter into the prepared pan and bake it at 350°F (177°C) for 20 to 25 minutes, or until a toothpick inserted in the middle comes out clean. Remove the brownies from the oven and allow them to cool for 5 minutes in the pan. Transfer the brownies to a baking rack and allow them to cool completely. I refrigerate them to speed up the cooling process, but you can allow them to cool at room temperature if you prefer.

When the brownies have cooled completely, cut them into ½-inch (1.3-cm) chunks.

(continued)

CHOCOLATE BROWNIE CHUNK (cont.)

For the Ice Cream

1 (14-oz [414-ml]) can sweetened condensed milk

1 tbsp (15 ml) pure vanilla extract

½ cup (120 ml) half-and-half

½ cup (50 g) Dutch-processed cocoa powder (unsweetened)

1½ cups (360 ml) heavy cream

In a medium-sized bowl, make the ice cream by whisking together the sweetened condensed milk, pure vanilla extract and half-and-half, until the mixture is smooth. Stir in the cocoa powder until no loose powder remains. Set this aside. With a standing or hand mixer, whip the heavy cream until stiff peaks form, 60 to 90 seconds. Fold the sweetened condensed milk mixture into the cream that has been whipped. This is your ice cream base. You will want this to be as smooth as possible and lump free. Fold in the cubed brownie pieces and ensure that they are evenly distributed throughout the ice cream base.

Pour the ice cream into an 8 x 8-inch (20 x 20–cm) baking pan (or a freezer-safe container of about the same size), and using your spatula, spread the ice cream evenly throughout the pan. Freeze the ice cream uncovered for 3 to 5 hours or overnight, until it is firm. Cover any leftovers with tinfoil or plastic wrap, and store them in the freezer for up to 3 weeks.

VARIATION: *If you prefer a spot of vanilla with your chocolate, mix those brownies into a Creamy Vanilla base (page 10). You could also swirl in some caramel (page 75) for a caramel brownie ice cream treat.*

ESPRESSO CHIP

This recipe yields roughly 12–14 standard scoops.

Espresso is like energy in a sweet, drinkable form. Its bold flavor is wonderful as it is, though some coffee lovers prefer to cut the taste with cream and sugar. This espresso chip ice cream is like a sweet frozen latte with a fun bite of chocolate throughout.

While my Bold Coffee ice cream (page 17) used real coffee extract to harness the flavor, I went a different route with this recipe. Real espresso powder + dark chocolate chips make this intense and deep, with flavor that's sure to give you more than a little pep in your step. Of course, if you prefer the decaf route, simply replace regular espresso powder with decaffeinated instant coffee and enjoy this treat well into the evening.

1 (14-oz [414-ml]) can sweetened condensed milk

2 tsp (10 ml) pure vanilla extract

2 tsp (9 g) espresso powder (regular or decaffeinated)

½ cup (120 ml) half-and-half

1½ cups (360 ml) heavy cream

1½ cups (248 g) dark chocolate chips

In a medium-sized bowl, whisk together the sweetened condensed milk, pure vanilla extract, espresso powder and half-and-half, until the mixture is smooth. Set this aside. With a standing or hand mixer, whip the heavy cream until stiff peaks form, 60 to 90 seconds. Fold the sweetened condensed milk mixture into the cream that has been whipped. This is your ice cream base. You will want this to be as smooth as possible and lump free. Fold in the chocolate chips, ensuring that they are evenly distributed throughout the ice cream.

Pour the ice cream into an 8 x 8-inch (20 x 20-cm) baking pan (or a freezer-safe container of about the same size), and using your spatula, spread the ice cream evenly throughout the pan. Freeze the ice cream uncovered for 3 to 5 hours or overnight, until it is firm. Cover any leftovers with tinfoil or plastic wrap, and store them in the freezer for up to 3 weeks.

VARIATION: If dark chocolate chips aren't your fancy, use your favorites! Milk chocolate, semi-sweet chocolate or even white chocolate chips would be delicious as mix-ins. Also, thoroughly stir in ¼ cup (25 g) of Dutch-processed cocoa powder and swirl in a helping of caramel sauce for a caramel mocha–like ice cream experience.

FUDGE BATTER SWIRL

This recipe yields roughly 12–14 standard scoops.

For the Fudge Batter Swirl

1¼ cups (206 g) semi-sweet chocolate chips

1 tbsp (14 g) salted butter

7 oz (207 ml) sweetened condensed milk

½ tsp pure vanilla extract

For the Ice Cream

1 (14-oz [414-ml]) can sweetened condensed milk

1 tbsp (15 ml) pure vanilla extract

½ cup (120 ml) half-and-half

1½ cups (360 ml) heavy cream

VARIATION: *How about peppermint fudge batter swirl? Add 1 teaspoon of pure peppermint extract to the base when adding the vanilla extract, and then continue as instructed.*

I love a good old fashioned fudge. This easy Fudge Batter Swirl is made with sweetened condensed milk (the same kind you will use in the ice cream base) and is only partially set up to ensure its swirl-ability into this fabulous classic vanilla ice cream. Enjoy taste testing along the way, as it's really a phenomenal fudge. You can double the fudge batter swirl recipe and use half to make real fudge alongside the ice cream—I fully support this route for maximum chocolate consumption.

In a medium-sized, microwave-safe bowl, make the fudge batter swirl by combining the chocolate chips, butter and sweetened condensed milk. Heat the mixture on high in the microwave for 1 minute. Cautiously remove the bowl from the microwave, as it could get hot while heating. Whisk the mixture and continue to heat it on high for 30-second increments until the mixture is completely melted and smooth. Stir in the pure vanilla extract. Place the mixture in the refrigerator to come to room temperature or slightly cooler, 10 to 15 minutes. You will want this mixture to be soft and pliable to swirl into the ice cream.

While the fudge batter swirl is chilling, make the ice cream base. In a medium-sized bowl, whisk together the sweetened condensed milk, pure vanilla extract and half-and-half, until it is smooth. Set this aside. With a standing or hand mixer, whip the heavy cream until stiff peaks form, 60 to 90 seconds. Fold the sweetened condensed milk mixture into the cream that has been whipped. This is your ice cream base. You will want this to be as smooth as possible and lump free.

Pour the ice cream into an 8 x 8-inch (20 x 20–cm) baking pan (or a freezer-safe container of about the same size), and using your spatula, spread the ice cream evenly throughout the pan. Remove the cooled fudge swirl from the refrigerator, and whisk to smooth out any spots that became slightly harder during the cooling process. Drop the fudge batter swirl by large tablespoons (15 ml) all over the ice cream base, ensuring that you cover the ice cream evenly and use the fudge mixture up. Using a butter knife, swirl the fudge batter througout the ice cream base. Freeze the ice cream uncovered for 3 to 5 hours or overnight, until it is firm. Cover any leftovers with tinfoil or plastic wrap, and store them in the freezer for up to 3 weeks.

IRISH CREAM FUDGE

This recipe yields roughly 12–14 standard scoops.

Irish cream is a flavor often associated with St. Patrick's Day, despite it not being a traditional Irish product. The flavor combines whiskey with cream and is generally added to cold drinks or coffee. Irish cream flavoring takes out the alcohol while leaving the flavor that comes from enjoying real Irish cream. Now, if you are looking to create an actual Irish cream ice cream with alcohol, you can definitely use the real thing. Just substitute about ¼ cup (60 ml) of real Irish cream for the flavoring (extracts and flavorings are generally more potent than their "real" counterparts).

This family-friendly version using a flavoring can be loved by all ages and is incorporated into a deep, rich fudge ice cream base.

1¼ cups (206 g) semi-sweet chocolate chips

1 tbsp (14 g) salted butter

1 (14-oz [414-ml]) can sweetened condensed milk

2 tsp (10 ml) pure vanilla extract

1 tbsp (15 ml) Irish cream flavoring or ¼ cup (60 ml) Irish cream

½ cup (120 ml) half-and-half

1½ cups (360 ml) heavy cream

VARIATION: *Create a dreamy coffee-inspired flavor combination by adding 1 tablespoon (15 ml) of pure coffee extract when adding the vanilla extract, and then continue as directed.*

In a medium-sized, microwave-safe bowl, combine the chocolate chips, butter and sweetened condensed milk. Heat the mixture on high in the microwave for 1 minute. Cautiously remove the bowl from the microwave, as it could get hot while heating. Whisk the mixture and continue to heat it on high for 30-second increments until the mixture is completely melted and smooth. Stir in the pure vanilla extract and Irish cream flavoring. Place the mixture in the refrigerator to just come to room temperature or slightly cooler, 10 to 15 minutes. You will want this mixture to be soft and pliable to swirl into the ice cream. This is your fudge batter base for the ice cream.

Remove the fudge batter base from the refrigerator and give it another good whisk. Add in the half-and-half and whisk well until everything is fully combined. Set this aside.

With a standing or hand mixer, whip the heavy cream until stiff peaks form, 60 to 90 seconds. Fold the fudge batter base into the cream that has been whipped. This is your ice cream base. You will want this to be as smooth as possible and lump free.

Pour the ice cream into an 8 x 8-inch (20 x 20-cm) baking pan (or a freezer-safe container of about the same size), and using your spatula, spread the ice cream evenly throughout the pan. Freeze the ice cream uncovered for 3 to 5 hours or overnight, until it is firm. Cover any leftovers with tinfoil or plastic wrap, and store them in the freezer for up to 3 weeks.

CREAMY KAHLUA

This recipe yields roughly 12–14 standard scoops.

1 (14-oz [414-ml]) can sweetened condensed milk

1 tbsp (15 ml) pure vanilla extract

1 tbsp (15 ml) Kahlua flavoring or ¼ cup (60 ml) Kahlua

½ cup (120 ml) half-and-half

1½ cups (360 ml) heavy cream

Kahlua was invented in Mexico in 1936. A couple of friends wondered what would happen if they added coffee to alcohol, and low and behold, Kahlua was born. Today, Kahlua consists of a combination of coffee (generally 100% Arabica coffee beans), rum, sugar and vanilla. I use a potent Kahlua flavoring to mimic the taste without the alcohol in this ice cream recipe.

Now, if you are looking to create an actual Kahlua cream ice cream with alcohol (similar to the Irish cream recipe on page 59), you can definitely use the real thing. Just substitute about ¼ cup (60 ml) of real Kahlua for the flavoring (extracts and flavorings are generally more potent than their "real" counterparts).

This family-friendly version using a flavoring can be loved by all ages, and is incorporated into a creamy, rich, vanilla ice cream base.

In a medium-sized bowl, whisk together the sweetened condensed milk, pure vanilla extract, Kahlua flavoring and half-and-half until the mixture is smooth. Set this aside. With a standing or hand mixer, whip the heavy cream until stiff peaks form, 60 to 90 seconds. Fold the sweetened condensed milk mixture into the cream that has been whipped. This is your ice cream base. You will want this to be as smooth as possible and lump free.

Pour the ice cream into an 8 x 8-inch (20 x 20-cm) baking pan (or a freezer-safe container of about the same size), and using your spatula, spread the ice cream evenly throughout the pan. Freeze the ice cream uncovered for 3 to 5 hours or overnight, until it is firm. Cover any leftovers with tinfoil or plastic wrap, and store them in the freezer for up to 3 weeks.

VARIATION: *Who loves mudslides? Let's turn this recipe into one by using ½ tablespoon (8 ml) of Kahlua, ½ tablespoon (8 ml) of Irish cream flavoring and swirling in ½ cup (120 ml) of Fudge Batter Swirl (page 56) or your favorite chocolate fudge sauce prior to freezing.*

On the Salty Side

In this chapter, we explore the salty side of desserts! And boy oh boy, do I have some good ones for you. Campfire S'mores (page 64) opens this section with a tried-and-true marshmallow fluff ice cream base (and SO MUCH milk chocolate + graham cracker chunks, it's not even funny). Toasted Coconut Crunch (page 72) brings the golden goodness of stovetop toasted coconut flakes mixed right into coconut ice cream. It's basically paradise without the palm trees.

I round out this chapter with Browned Butter Caramel Walnut (page 78) and what can I say, except OH GOODNESS, IT IS A MUST TRY. Real browned butter and every single glorious fleck of flavor is packed into this buttery, completely mesmerizing concoction.

Strap yourself in, because the salty side is going to come in hot.

CAMPFIRE S'MORES

This recipe yields roughly 12–14 standard scoops.

1 (14-oz [414-ml]) can sweetened condensed milk

1 (7-oz [198-g]) container marshmallow fluff

2 tsp (10 ml) pure vanilla extract

½ cup (120 ml) half-and-half

1½ cups (360 ml) heavy cream

2 cups (338 g) graham pieces (I use Annie's® Honey Bunny Grahams)

1 (4.4-oz [125-g]) bar Lindt® milk chocolate, chopped

S'mores evoke the very essence of summertime. There's something so nostalgic about sitting around a campfire, roasting a marshmallow until it is toasty and golden, and sandwiching it in between two graham crackers with a nice big hunk of milk chocolate. It's gooey, warm and satisfying to no end.

We mimic that glorious s'mores flavor in this ice cream recipe by adding real marshmallow fluff to the base and plenty of milk chocolate + graham crackers as add-ins. No camping is required, but it would be pretty cozy to enjoy a big bowl of this s'mores ice cream around a glowing fire.

In a medium-sized bowl, whisk together the sweetened condensed milk, marshmallow fluff, pure vanilla extract and half-and-half, until the mixture is smooth. Set this aside. With a standing or hand mixer, whip the heavy cream until stiff peaks form, 60 to 90 seconds. Fold the sweetened condensed milk mixture into the cream that has been whipped. This is your ice cream base. You will want this to be as smooth as possible and lump free. Fold in the graham pieces and the chopped milk chocolate, reserving about ¼ cup of each (42 g graham pieces and 31 g chocolate) to sprinkle over the top. This is optional—you can mix it all in if you prefer.

Pour the ice cream into an 8 x 8-inch (20 x 20-cm) baking pan (or a freezer-safe container of about the same size), and using your spatula, spread the ice cream evenly throughout the pan. Freeze the ice cream uncovered for 3 to 5 hours or overnight, until it is firm. Generously sprinkle on the graham pieces and chocolate you set aside earlier. Cover any leftovers with tinfoil or plastic wrap, and store them in the freezer for up to 3 weeks.

VARIATION: *Have you ever made a s'more with a peanut butter cup? It's incredible! Mimic that flavor combination by adding 1 cup (250 g) of chopped peanut butter cups to the mix-ins in this recipe. Also, try scooping this ice cream out and sandwiching it between two graham crackers . . . It's phenomenal.*

DULCE DE LECHE

This recipe yields roughly 12–14 standard scoops.

Dulce de leche is simply caramelized milk plus sugar. It is divine in cakes, cookies and an array of other desserts. There are various methods for making it yourself (one of which involves heating a can of sweetened condensed milk). I've simplified this process by using a can of already caramelized sweetened condensed milk in this amazingly creamy recipe. Notes of pure vanilla extract come though as well in this astonishingly easy no-churn ice cream.

1 (13.4-oz [395-ml]) can La Lechera Dulce de Leche

2 tsp (10 ml) pure vanilla extract

½ cup (120 ml) half-and-half

1½ cups (360 ml) heavy cream

In a medium-sized bowl, whisk together the Dulce de Leche, pure vanilla extract and half-and-half, until the mixture is smooth. Set this aside. With a standing or hand mixer, whip the heavy cream until stiff peaks form, 60 to 90 seconds. Fold the sweetened condensed milk mixture into the cream that has been whipped. This is your ice cream base. You will want this to be as smooth as possible and lump free.

Pour the ice cream into an 8 x 8–inch (20 x 20–cm) baking pan (or a freezer-safe container of about the same size), and using your spatula, spread the ice cream evenly throughout the pan. Freeze the ice cream uncovered for 3 to 5 hours or overnight, until it is firm. Cover any leftovers with tinfoil or plastic wrap, and store them in the freezer for up to 3 weeks.

VARIATION: *A swirl of homemade caramel would be outrageously satisfying in this milky caramel-based ice cream. Simply make the recipe from page 75 and swirl it in before freezing as instructed.*

CHUNKY ROCKY ROAD

This recipe yields roughly 12–14 standard scoops.

1 (14-oz [414-ml]) can sweetened condensed milk

1 tbsp (15 ml) pure vanilla extract

½ cup (120 ml) half-and-half

½ cup (50 g) Dutch-processed cocoa powder (unsweetened)

1½ cups (360 ml) heavy cream

2 cups (100 g) mini marshmallows

1 cup (146 g) walnuts, chopped

Rich chocolate, mini marshmallows and chopped walnuts blend together seamlessly in this ultra-popular ice cream flavor. I give specifics on how much of each ingredient to add when it comes to marshmallows and nuts, but you can add more if you love a super chunky ice cream, or less if you'd like just a little of this flavor combination. There is no wrong way to enjoy Chunky Rocky Road, especially one as quick and easy as this no-churn variety.

In a medium-sized bowl, whisk together the sweetened condensed milk, pure vanilla extract and half-and-half, until the mixture is smooth. Stir in the cocoa powder until no loose powder remains. Set this aside. With a standing or hand mixer, whip the heavy cream until stiff peaks form, 60 to 90 seconds. Fold the sweetened condensed milk mixture into the cream that has been whipped. This is your ice cream base. You will want this to be as smooth as possible and lump free. Fold in the mini marshmallows and the walnuts, ensuring that there is an even distribution throughout the ice cream base.

Pour the ice cream into an 8 x 8–inch (20 x 20–cm) baking pan (or a freezer-safe container of about the same size), and using your spatula, spread the ice cream evenly throughout the pan. Freeze the ice cream uncovered for 3 to 5 hours or overnight, until it is firm. Cover any leftovers with tinfoil or plastic wrap, and store them in the freezer for up to 3 weeks.

VARIATION: *Not a walnut lover? Replace this nut with your favorite nuts such as peanuts, almonds or pecans, all of which have appeared in various rocky road recipes around the globe.*

SEA SALT HONEY NUT

This recipe yields roughly 12–14 standard scoops.

I use real raw honey to compliment buttery walnuts and Fleur de Sel in this completely tantalizing no-churn ice cream flavor. It is perfectly sweet and perfectly salty, marrying the best of both worlds into one easy recipe.

1 (14-oz [414-ml]) can sweetened condensed milk

2 tsp (10 ml) pure vanilla extract

½ cup (120 ml) half-and-half

1½ cups (360 ml) heavy cream

⅔ cup (97 g) walnuts, chopped

⅓ cup (80 ml) raw honey

1 tsp Fleur de Sel or sea salt

In a medium-sized bowl, whisk together the sweetened condensed milk, pure vanilla extract and half-and-half, until the mixture is smooth. Set this aside. With a standing or hand mixer, whip the heavy cream until stiff peaks form, 60 to 90 seconds. Fold the sweetened condensed milk mixture into the cream that has been whipped. This is your ice cream base. You will want this to be as smooth as possible and lump free. Fold in the chopped walnuts, ensuring that they are evenly disturbed throughout the ice cream base.

Pour a half of the ice cream into an 8 x 8–inch (20 x 20–cm) baking pan (or a freezer-safe container of about the same size), and using your spatula, spread the ice cream evenly throughout the pan. With a teaspoon, drizzle half of the honey over the ice cream as evenly as possible. Sprinkle half of the fleur de sel evenly over the honey drizzled base. Pour the remaining half of the ice cream base into the pan and drizzle the remaining honey over the top of the ice cream. Sprinkle the rest of the fleur de sel on top. With a butter knife or fork, gently swirl the honey and fleur de sel around into the ice cream, ensuring that you do not over mix it. You will want those sweet pockets of salted honey drizzle to come through once frozen. Freeze the ice cream uncovered for 3 to 5 hours or overnight, until it is firm. Cover any leftovers with tinfoil or plastic wrap, and store them in the freezer for up to 3 weeks.

Note: If you don't love a strong sea salt flavor, but wish to try it out, simply omit the salt in the recipe and sprinkle a little bit over a scoop once it is ready to eat. That way you can see how much you enjoy in this salty treat.

VARIATION: *Not a fan of Fleur de Sel or sea salt? Omit it and enjoy this sweet honey nut ice cream sans the addition of salt.*

TOASTED COCONUT CRUNCH

This recipe yields roughly 12–14 standard scoops.

1 cup (93 g) unsweetened coconut flakes

1 (14-oz [414-ml]) can sweetened condensed milk

2 tsp (10 ml) pure vanilla extract

2 tsp (10 ml) pure coconut extract paste or pure coconut extract

½ cup (120 ml) half-and-half

1½ cups (360 ml) heavy cream

While the origin of the coconut remains somewhat a mystery to many scholars, today we tend to equate it with white sand beaches, beautiful blue oceans and palm trees aplenty.

Fortunately, you do not need to hop a plane to the closest tropical destination to enjoy truly magnificent coconut ice cream. I begin with a pure coconut extract paste mixed right into the base, and then add plenty of toasted coconut flakes for that irreplaceable texture. If you cannot find a coconut paste, pure coconut extract will work just fine at the same measurement as the paste.

Now if you prefer the flavor of coconut, but don't necessary want the crunch, you can blend the toasted coconut with about 1 cup (240 ml) of the ice cream base in a blender until it is smooth. Pour this mixture back into the rest of the base and you've got the same toasted coconut flavor minus the texture of the flakes.

Begin by toasting the coconut flakes. Place the unsweetened coconut in a medium saucepan on the stovetop over medium to high heat. You will want to watch this the entire time because it can burn easily. Whisk the coconut flakes while they warm up. This ensures an even distribution of heat and a golden texture throughout. Once the coconut has become a medium golden color, immediately remove it from the heat. Pour it into another bowl to stop the cooking process. Place the bowl of toasted coconut in the refrigerator to cool off for about 10 minutes.

In a medium-sized bowl, whisk together the sweetened condensed milk, pure vanilla extract, pure coconut extract paste and half-and-half, until the mixture is smooth. Set this aside. With a standing or hand mixer, whip the heavy cream until stiff peaks form, 60 to 90 seconds. Fold the sweetened condensed milk mixture into the cream that has been whipped. This is your ice cream base. You will want this to be as smooth as possible, and lump free.

(continued)

TOASTED COCONUT CRUNCH (cont.)

Gently fold in the cooled toasted coconut flakes, ensuring they are evenly distributed throughout the ice cream base.

Pour the ice cream into an 8 x 8-inch (20 x 20-cm) baking pan (or a freezer-safe container of about the same size), and using your spatula, spread the ice cream evenly throughout the pan. Freeze the ice cream uncovered for 3 to 5 hours or overnight, until it is firm. Cover any leftovers with tinfoil or plastic wrap, and store them in the freezer for up to 3 weeks.

VARIATION: *This recipe is absolutely fabulous in an ice cream sandwich. Bake up a batch of coconut shortbread cookies to sandwich them between using the recipe from the Blueberry Pie on page 117. Add 1 teaspoon of pure coconut extract or pure coconut extract paste to the dough when adding the vanilla, and then continue as instructed. Sandwich the cookies per the instructions on page 132, and enjoy an even more tropical experience.*

TURTLE (CHOCOLATE CARAMEL PECAN)

This recipe yields roughly 12–14 standard scoops.

This turtle ice cream starts with my no-churn Creamy Vanilla ice cream base (page 10). Turtle candies are chopped and added to the mix, along with a generous ripple of homemade caramel. Now this caramel is a cinch to put together, and only requires three ingredients for maximum flavor with nothing artificial. If you wish to use store-bought caramel, you can substitute that in at a one-to-one ratio. Try to choose a store-bought caramel that is made with a brief ingredient list to best mimic the flavor of homemade caramel.

For the Caramel

½ cup (100 g) granulated sugar

¼ cup (57 g) salted butter

¼ cup (60 ml) heavy cream

To make the caramel, place the granulated sugar in a small saucepan on the stovetop over medium to high heat. Whisk the sugar continuously without stopping until it is melted. Be very cautious as you do not want the sugar to burn and be aware of splatter as well. It will be extremely hot!

Once the sugar reduces to a dark amber-colored liquid, about 3 to 5 minutes, add the butter. Whisk this bubbly liquid until it is fully combined and no lumps remain. Lower the heat to a simmer. Slowly add the heavy cream and mix the caramel, until it is well combined. Remove the pan from the heat and allow the caramel to cool completely. The caramel will thicken as it cools. If your mixture clumps up at all, simply pop the pan back onto the burner, and then turn the heat up to medium for a minute or two of vigorous stirring. It will come together.

You can place the pan in the refrigerator to speed up the cooling process. I generally allow my caramel to cool for 45 to 60 minutes. You will use all of this caramel in this recipe, but should you choose to double it and have some extra, you can store any leftovers in an airtight glass container for up to 1 month in the refrigerator. You can warm the caramel to loosen it up after it has been refrigerated, as it will stiffen. The caramel is still pliable though, so it can be eaten warm or cold.

(continued)

TURTLE (CHOCOLATE CARAMEL PECAN) (cont.)

In a medium-sized bowl, make the ice cream by whisking together the sweetened condensed milk, pure vanilla extract and half-and-half, until it is smooth. Set this aside. With a standing or hand mixer, whip the heavy cream until stiff peaks form, 60 to 90 seconds. Fold the sweetened condensed milk mixture into the cream that has been whipped. This is your ice cream base. You will want this to be as smooth as possible and lump free. Add the chopped turtle candies to the base and fold them in with a spatula. Ensure that they are well distributed throughout the ice cream.

Pour half of the ice cream base into an 8 x 8–inch (20 x 20–cm) baking pan (or a freezer-safe container of about the same size), and using your spatula, spread the ice cream evenly throughout the pan. Using half of the prepared and cooled caramel, spoon large tablespoons (15 ml) over the ice cream base. Pour the remaining half of the ice cream base into the pan, and finally, drizzle the remaining caramel over the ice cream base. Using a butter knife or fork, gently swirl the caramel into the base, ensuring that you do not overmix it. You'll want those delightful pockets of caramel to be present throughout the ice cream. Freeze the ice cream uncovered for 3 to 5 hours or overnight, until it is firm. Cover any leftovers with tinfoil or plastic wrap, and store them in the freezer for up to 3 weeks.

VARIATION: *These mix-ins would be fabulous in both the Rich Chocolate recipe (page 13), or the Caramel Peanut Crunch Ice Cream Bars (page 129) sans peanuts.*

For the Ice Cream

1 (14-oz [414-ml]) can sweetened condensed milk

2 tsp (10 ml) pure vanilla extract

½ cup (120 ml) half-and-half

1½ cups (360 ml) heavy cream

2 cups (292 g) turtle candies, chopped

BROWNED BUTTER CARAMEL WALNUT

This recipe yields roughly 12–14 standard scoops.

For the Caramel

½ cup (100 g) granulated sugar

¼ cup (57 g) salted butter

¼ cup (60 ml) heavy cream

This ice cream flavor encompasses many of my favorite things. Gloriously browned and cooled butter lends its nutty flavor and aroma to a creamy vanilla base. Homemade caramel is swirled throughout, and toasted walnuts complete this incredibly decadent ice cream.

As with the Turtle (Chocolate Caramel Pecan) ice cream recipe (page 75), you can substitute store-bought caramel for this homemade version. Try to choose a store-bought caramel that is made with a brief ingredient list to best mimic the flavor of homemade caramel. When using storebought caramel, about 1 cup (236 ml) does the trick.

To make the caramel, place the granulated sugar in a small saucepan on the stovetop, over medium to high heat. Whisk the sugar continuously without stopping, until it is melted. Be very cautious, as you do not want the sugar to burn, and be aware of splatter as well. It will be extremely hot!

Once the sugar reduces to a dark amber-colored liquid, about 3 to 5 minutes, add the butter. Whisk this bubbly liquid until it is fully combined and no lumps remain. Lower the heat to a simmer.

Slowly add the heavy cream and mix the caramel, until it is well combined. Remove the pan from the heat and allow the caramel to cool completely. The caramel will thicken as it cools. If your mixture clumps up at all, simply pop the pan back onto the burner and then turn the heat up to medium for a minute or two of vigorous stirring. It will come together.

(continued)

For the Ice Cream

½ cup (73 g) walnuts, chopped

2 tbsp (28 g) salted butter, browned and cooled

1 (14-oz [414-ml]) can sweetened condensed milk

2 tsp (10 ml) pure vanilla extract

½ cup (120 ml) half-and-half

1½ cups (360 ml) heavy cream

You can place the pan in the refrigerator to speed up the cooling process. I generally allow my caramel to cool for 45 to 60 minutes. You will use all of this caramel in this recipe, but should you choose to double it and have some extra, you can store any leftovers in an airtight glass container for up to 1 month in the refrigerator. You can warm the caramel to loosen it up after it has been refrigerated, as it will stiffen. It is still pliable though, so it can be eaten warm or cold.

Before you add them to the ice cream, you will want to toast the walnuts and brown the butter first to allow both of these ingredients to cool down completely.

Preheat the oven to 350°F (177°C). On a small baking sheet or cookie sheet, spread the walnuts out. Place them in the oven and toast them for 7 minutes, or until they are slightly more golden and fragrant. Remove the walnuts from the oven and allow them to cool completely.

In a small saucepan, add the salted butter. Place the saucepan on the stovetop over medium heat. As the butter starts to melt and bubble, be cautious of any splatter as it could be hot. Whisk the butter as it browns, ensuring that you remove it from the heat as soon as it hits a nice deep golden color, about 2 to 5 minutes. Pour the browned butter into a small bowl to stop the cooking process, and then place the bowl in the refrigerator for the butter to chill. After about 10 minutes, the butter should be cooled and resemble the consistency of a paste. Give the butter a good whisk to ensure that you get all of the golden-brown specks mixed in (these tend to settle at the bottom of the bowl).

In a medium-sized bowl, whisk together the sweetened condensed milk, pure vanilla extract, browned butter and half-and-half, until the mixture is smooth. Set this aside. With a standing or hand mixer, whip the heavy cream until stiff peaks form, 60 to 90 seconds. Fold the sweetened condensed milk mixture into the cream that has been whipped. This is your ice cream base. You will want this to be as smooth as possible and lump free. Fold in the cooled toasted walnuts.

Pour half of the ice cream base into an 8 x 8-inch (20 x 20–cm) baking pan (or a freezer-safe container of about the same size), and using your spatula, spread the ice cream evenly throughout the pan. Using half of the prepared and cooled caramel, spoon large tablespoons (15 ml) over the ice cream base. Pour the remaining half of the ice cream base into the pan, and finally, drizzle the remaining caramel over the ice cream base. Using a butter knife or fork, gently swirl the caramel into the base, ensuring that you do not overmix it. You'll want those delightful pockets of caramel to be present throughout the ice cream. Freeze the ice cream uncovered for 3 to 5 hours or overnight, until it is firm. Cover any leftovers with tinfoil or plastic wrap, and store them in the freezer for up to 3 weeks.

VARIATION: *Substitute your favorite nut if walnuts aren't your thing, or simply omit them altogether. This base will shine with or without those little nuts.*

Cookies + Cheesecakes

There are few things more irresistible than a cheesecake. In this chapter, we explore how no-churn cheesecake ice cream can be fruity, salty and pumpkin-y. Also, cookies are not to be discounted, as four recipes call for a variety of them mixed right in. From speculoos (page 84), to oatmeal raisin (page 87), to downright delicious edible cookie dough (page 89), there's no shortage of baked goods swirled right into this no-churn ice cream goodness.

COOKIE BUTTER SWIRL

This recipe yields roughly 12–14 standard scoops.

1 (14-oz [414-ml]) can sweetened condensed milk

1 tbsp (15 ml) vanilla bean paste or pure vanilla extract

½ cup (120 ml) half-and-half

1½ cups (360 ml) heavy cream

15 Biscoff cookies, crushed into varying small-sized pieces

½ cup (148 g) Biscoff cookie butter

Believe it or not, I spent the majority of my childhood and adult life not really knowing what cookie butter was. I first tried it about 3 years ago and became instantly hooked. A blend of speculoos cookie plus a variety of other ingredients create the creamiest and most luscious spread that we know as cookie butter. It is fantastic on toast, in cake fillings and even in cheesecakes. This cookie butter swirl ice cream, however, takes the top spot.

There are a variety of brands out there that are all delicious, but for this recipe, I stuck with the Biscoff® brand. You will use both the Biscoff cookie butter and crushed Biscoff cookies to bring this recipe to life. A strong paste is used to intensify the vanilla flavor and perfectly complement the cookie butter. If you cannot find vanilla bean paste, you can use pure vanilla extract at the same measurement.

In a medium-sized bowl, whisk together the sweetened condensed milk, vanilla bean paste and half-and-half, until the mixture is smooth. Set this aside. With a standing or hand mixer, whip the heavy cream until stiff peaks form, 60 to 90 seconds. Gently fold the sweetened condensed milk mixture into the cream that has been whipped. This is your ice cream base. You will want this to be as smooth as possible and lump free.

Add the crushed Biscoff cookies, and gently mix with a spatula to ensure an even distribution throughout the ice cream. Pour the ice cream into an 8 x 8–inch (20 x 20–cm) baking pan, and using your spatula, spread it evenly throughout the pan. Drop spoonfuls of cookie butter all over the top of the ice cream and swirl the cookie butter into the ice cream with a butter knife. Do not overmix, as you want those delicious pockets of cookie butter to be present once the ice cream is ready. Freeze the ice cream uncovered for 3 to 5 hours or overnight, until it is firm. Cover any leftovers with tinfoil or plastic wrap, and store them in the freezer for up to 2 weeks.

VARIATION: *If you'd like actual cookie butter mixed right into the base, whisk ¼ cup (74 g) of cookie butter into the sweetened condensed milk and cream mixture before folding in the whipped cream. Continue with the recipe as instructed.*

OATMEAL RAISIN COOKIE

This recipe yields roughly 12–14 standard scoops.

The oatmeal raisin cookie gained popularity due to being labeled as a health food when they first hit the market. Although definitely classified as a dessert today, these flavor-packed goodies have remained one of the most popular cookies available. For this ice cream recipe, a small batch of classic oatmeal cookies are baked to perfection, cooled and then crumbled into delicious cinnamon–vanilla bean no-churn ice cream.

To make the cookies, begin by preheating the oven to 350°F (177°C). In a medium-sized bowl, combine the butter and both sugars. Cream this well by hand, or with a standing or handheld mixer. Add the egg and beat well for about 15 seconds. Add in the pure vanilla extract, flour, baking soda, salt, cinnamon and nutmeg. Mix until well incorporated, for about 30 seconds.

Fold in the oats and the raisins, until they are evenly distributed throughout the dough. Drop the dough by 2-tablespoon (30-ml) scoops onto a parchment paper–lined cookie sheet. This will help prevent the cookies from sticking to the cookie sheet. You can also use a nonstick baking sheet if you prefer to eliminate the use of the parchment paper.

Bake the cookies for 8 to 10 minutes, or until they are golden on the outside. Remove them from the oven and allow them to cool on the baking sheet for about 1 minute before moving the cookies to a wire rack to cool completely. You will want them room temperature before you add them to the ice cream base.

(continued)

For the Cookies

½ cup (114 g) salted butter, softened

½ cup (110 g) firmly packed dark brown sugar

2 tbsp (25 g) granulated sugar

1 large egg

1 tsp pure vanilla extract

¾ cup (96 g) all-purpose flour

½ tsp baking soda

¼ tsp salt

1 tsp ground cinnamon

¼ tsp ground nutmeg

1½ cups (120 g) quick or old fashioned oats, uncooked

¾ cup (109 g) raisins

OATMEAL RAISIN COOKIE (cont.)

For the Ice Cream

1 (14-oz [414-ml]) can sweetened condensed milk

2 tsp (10 ml) pure vanilla extract

2 tsp (5 g) ground cinnamon

½ cup (120 ml) half-and-half

1½ cups (360 ml) heavy cream

In a medium-sized bowl, make the ice cream by whisking together the sweetened condensed milk, pure vanilla extract, cinnamon and half-and-half, until the mixture is smooth. Set this aside. With a standing or hand mixer, whip the heavy cream until stiff peaks form, 60 to 90 seconds. Fold the sweetened condensed milk mixture into the cream that has been whipped. This is your ice cream base. You will want this to be as smooth as possible and lump free.

Crumble the cooled oatmeal raisin cookies into about 1-inch (2.5-cm) chunks. Fold the cookie pieces into the ice cream base.

Pour the ice cream into an 8 x 8-inch (20 x 20–cm) baking pan (or a freezer-safe container of about the same size), and using your spatula, spread the ice cream evenly throughout the pan. Freeze the ice cream uncovered for 3 to 5 hours or overnight, until it is firm. Cover any leftovers with tinfoil or plastic wrap, and store them in the freezer for up to 3 weeks.

VARIATION: *If raisins aren't your thing, sub in chocolate chips for the raisins to make oatmeal chocolate chip cookies for this recipe instead.*

COOKIE DOUGH CHUNKS

This recipe yields roughly 12–14 standard scoops.

Edible cookie dough is packed into no-churn vanilla ice cream for a truly delightful treat. There are no tiny pieces of dough here—you can add as much or as little of the cookie dough as you see fit. And don't forget to sample as you go—this cookie dough is egg-free and we microwave the flour for a completely safe dough-eating experience. This ice cream is perfect for the whole family and easy enough for kids to help with! Pull up a spoon and enjoy.

It is best to make the cookie dough first, as it needs about 20 minutes of refrigeration before it is added to the ice cream. Making the ice cream is step two, but by all means, reverse the steps if you'd like to enjoy some tantalizing cookie dough before or while you make the ice cream!

In a small to medium-sized bowl, cream the butter and both sugars together with a wooden spoon, until it is smooth. Add in the heavy cream, pure vanilla extract and salt. Blend the ingredients until everything is incorporated. Add the flour and mix well, finally folding the mini chocolate chips into the batter. Drop the dough by small teaspoonfuls onto a parchment paper lined cookie sheet, and refrigerate it for 20 minutes or until the dough is solid. These cookie dough "bites" will be added to the ice cream base.

In a medium-sized bowl, make the ice cream by whisking together the sweetened condensed milk, vanilla extract and half-and-half, until the mixture is smooth. Set this aside. With a standing or hand mixer, whip the heavy cream until stiff peaks form, 60 to 90 seconds. Gently fold the sweetened condensed milk mixture into the cream that has been whipped. This is your ice cream base. You will want this to be as smooth as possible and lump free.

(continued)

For the Edible Cookie Dough

½ cup (114 g) salted butter, softened

¼ cup (50 g) granulated sugar

½ cup (110 g) firmly packed brown sugar

2 tbsp (30 ml) heavy cream

1 tsp pure vanilla extract

½ tsp salt

1¼ cups (160 g) all-purpose flour*

¾ cup (124 g) mini chocolate chips

For the Ice Cream

1 (14-oz [414-ml]) can sweetened condensed milk

1 tbsp (15 ml) pure vanilla extract

½ cup (120 ml) half-and-half

1½ cups (360 ml) heavy cream

COOKIE DOUGH CHUNKS (cont.)

It has been said that there is a small risk of E. coli when consuming raw flour. If this concerns you, microwave your flour for 1 minute and 15 seconds, or until a temperature of 160°F (71°C) is reached. Allow the flour to cool completely and then proceed with the recipe.

After 20 minutes, remove the cookie dough bites from the refrigerator and mix them gently into the ice cream base with a spatula or wooden spoon. Pour the ice cream into a 8 x 8–inch (20 x 20–cm) baking pan (or a freezer-safe container of about the same size), using a spatula to spread it evenly throughout the pan. Freeze the ice cream uncovered for 3 to 5 hours or overnight, until it is firm. Cover any leftovers with tinfoil or plastic wrap, and store them in the freezer for up to 3 weeks.

VARIATION: *If you love peanut butter and cookie dough, add a ½ cup (129 g) of creamy peanut butter to the base, and continue making the recipe as instructed.*

BLACKBERRY CHEESECAKE

This recipe yields roughly 12–14 standard scoops.

This delightful cheesecake ice cream base uses fresh cream cheese to yield an incredible cheesecake flavor. The addition of a fresh blackberry sauce ripples its way throughout the ice cream, ensuring that you absolutely cannot miss this sweet, tart and divinely creamy combination.

To make the blackberry sauce, begin by placing the blackberries, granulated sugar, cornstarch and fresh lemon juice in a medium-sized saucepan. Place the pan on the stovetop over medium-high heat. Using a potato masher, begin to mash the fruit and ingredients, until they come together as the mixture starts to warm up. After 1 to 2 minutes of cooking, the mixture will begin to bubble. Lower the heat to medium, and stir frequently, until the fruit sauce thickens, another 1 to 2 minutes. Remove the mixture from the heat, and transfer to a bowl. Refrigerate until completely cool, about 30 minutes.

In a medium-sized bowl, make the ice cream by whisking together the softened cream cheese, until it is light and fluffy, about 1 minute. Add the sweetened condensed milk, half-and-half and vanilla extract. Whisk until all ingredients are thoroughly combined. Set this aside. With a standing or hand mixer, whip the heavy cream until stiff peaks form, 60 to 90 seconds. Fold the sweetened condensed milk mixture into the cream that has been whipped. This is your ice cream base. You will want this to be as smooth as possible and lump free.

Pour the ice cream into an 8 x 8–inch (20 x 20–cm) baking pan (or a freezer-safe container of about the same size), and using your spatula, spread the ice cream evenly throughout the pan. Remove the blackberry sauce mixture from the refrigerator. Drop the mixture by full tablespoons (15 ml) all over the top of the ice cream base, using all of it up. Take a butter knife or fork, and swirl the mixture into the base, ensuring that it is dispersed throughout the ice cream. Freeze the ice cream uncovered for 3 to 5 hours or overnight, until it is firm. Cover any leftovers with tinfoil or plastic wrap, and store them in the freezer for up to 3 weeks.

For the Blackberry Sauce

2 cups (246 g) fresh blackberries

½ cup (100 g) granulated sugar

2 tbsp (16 g) cornstarch

2 tbsp (30 ml) fresh squeezed lemon juice

For the Ice Cream

4 oz (113 g) cream cheese, softened to room temperature

1 (14-oz [414-ml]) can sweetened condensed milk

½ cup (120 ml) half-and-half

1 tbsp (15 ml) pure vanilla extract

1½ cups (360 ml) heavy cream

VARIATION: *Substitute your favorite berry here if you prefer another over blackberries! It's a one-to-one substitute, so choose your berry and make as instructed.*

COFFEE CARAMEL COOKIE

This recipe yields roughly 12–14 standard scoops.

For the Caramel

½ cup (100 g) granulated sugar

¼ cup (57 g) salted butter

¼ cup (60 ml) heavy cream

In this tantalizing blend of coffee-flavored ice cream, ripples of homemade caramel and crushed chocolate sandwich cookies, we find decadence personified. Strong and pure coffee extract lends its bold flavor to the ice cream base, and a generous caramel swirl weaves in and out of hearty cookie chunks.

As with the Turtle (Chocolate Caramel Pecan) (page 75) and Browned Butter Caramel Walnut (page 78) ice cream recipes, you can substitute store-bought caramel for this homemade version if you need to. Try to choose a store-bought caramel that is made with minimal ingredients to best mimic the flavor of homemade caramel. When using storebought caramel, about 1 cup (236 ml) does the trick.

To make the caramel, begin by placing the granulated sugar in a small saucepan on the stovetop, over medium to high heat. Whisk the sugar continuously without stopping, until it is melted. Be very cautious, as you do not want the sugar to burn, and be aware of splatter. It will be extremely hot!

Once the sugar reduces to a dark amber-colored liquid, about 3 to 5 minutes, add the butter. Whisk this bubbly liquid until it is fully combined and no lumps remain. Lower the heat to a simmer. Slowly add the heavy cream and mix the caramel, until it is well combined. Remove the pan from the heat and allow the caramel to cool completely. The caramel will thicken as it cools. If your mixture clumps up at all, simply pop the pan back onto the burner, and then turn the heat up to medium for 1 or 2 minutes of vigorous stirring. It will come together.

You can place the pan in the refrigerator to speed up the cooling process. I generally allow my caramel to cool for 45 to 60 minutes. You will use all of this caramel in this recipe, but should you choose to double it and have some extra, you can store any leftovers in an airtight glass container for up to 1 month in the refrigerator. You can warm the caramel to loosen it up after it has been refrigerated, as it will stiffen. It is still pliable though, so it can be eaten warm or cold.

(continued)

COFFEE CARAMEL COOKIE (cont.)

For the Ice Cream

1 (14-oz [414-ml]) can sweetened condensed milk

1 tbsp (15 ml) pure vanilla extract

1 tbsp (15 ml) pure coffee extract

½ cup (120 ml) half-and-half

1½ cups (360 ml) heavy cream

15 chocolate sandwich cookies (I used Oreos)

In a medium-sized bowl, make the ice cream by whisking together the sweetened condensed milk, pure vanilla extract, pure coffee extract and half-and-half, until the mixture is smooth. Set this aside. With a standing or hand mixer, whip the heavy cream until stiff peaks form, 60 to 90 seconds. Fold the sweetened condensed milk mixture into the cream that has been whipped. This is your ice cream base. You will want this to be as smooth as possible and lump free.

Place the sandwich cookies in a large sturdy plastic bag and seal it, ensuring most of the air has been removed. Using a rolling pin, roll over the cookies to break them up into larger chunks. Alternatively, you can crush them by hand, breaking each cookie roughly into fourths. If you prefer smaller chunks, simply crush the cookies further. If you prefer larger chunks, crush them less. Place the crushed cookies into the ice cream mixture, and gently mix, ensuring that the cookies are well distributed within the batch of ice cream.

Pour half of the ice cream base into an 8 x 8–inch (20 x 20–cm) baking pan (or a freezer-safe container of about the same size), and using your spatula, spread the ice cream evenly throughout the pan. Using half of the prepared and cooled caramel, spoon large tablespoons (15 ml) over the ice cream base. Pour the remaining half of the ice cream base into the pan, and finally, drizzle the remaining caramel over the ice cream base. Using a butter knife or fork, gently swirl the caramel into the base, ensuring that you do not overmix it. You'll want those delightful pockets of caramel to be present throughout the ice cream. Freeze the ice cream uncovered for 3 to 5 hours or overnight, until it is firm. Cover any leftovers with tinfoil or plastic wrap, and store them in the freezer for up to 3 weeks.

VARIATION: *If coffee isn't your love language, you can omit it for a delicious vanilla ice cream with caramel and Oreos.*

CARAMEL CHEESECAKE RIPPLE

This recipe yields roughly 12–14 standard scoops.

We use the same cheesecake base in this caramel cheesecake ripple ice cream, and let me tell you, the combination of cheesecake and homemade caramel sauce is truly out of this world.

As with the several previous ice cream recipes in this book, you can substitute store-bought caramel for this homemade version if you need to. Try to choose a store-bought caramel that is made with minimal ingredients to best mimic the flavor of homemade caramel. When using storebought caramel, about 1 cup (236 ml) does the trick.

For the Caramel

½ cup (100 g) granulated sugar

¼ cup (57 g) salted butter

¼ cup (60 ml) heavy cream

To make the caramel, place the granulated sugar in a small saucepan on the stovetop over medium to high heat. Whisk the sugar continuously without stopping, until it is melted. Be very cautious, as you do not want the sugar to burn, and be aware of splatter. It will be extremely hot!

Once the sugar reduces to a dark amber-colored liquid, about 3 to 5 minutes, add the butter. Whisk this bubbly liquid until it is fully combined and no lumps remain. Lower the heat to a simmer. Slowly add the heavy cream and mix the caramel, until it is well combined. Remove the pan from the heat and allow the caramel to cool completely. The caramel will thicken as it cools. If your mixture clumps up at all, simply pop the pan back onto the burner and then turn the heat up to medium for 1 or 2 minutes of vigorous stirring. It will come together.

You can place the pan in the refrigerator to speed up the cooling process. I generally allow my caramel to cool for 45 to 60 minutes. You will use all of this caramel in this recipe, but should you choose to double it and have some extra. You can store any leftovers in an airtight glass container for up to 1 month in the refrigerator. You can warm the caramel to loosen it up after it has been refrigerated, as it will stiffen. It is still pliable though, so it can be eaten warm or cold.

(continued)

CARAMEL CHEESECAKE RIPPLE (cont.)

In a medium-sized bowl, make the ice cream by whisking the softened cream cheese until it is light and fluffy, about 1 minute. Add in the sweetened condensed milk, half-and-half and vanilla extract. Whisk until combined. Set this aside. With a standing or hand mixer, whip the heavy cream until stiff peaks form, 60 to 90 seconds. Fold the sweetened condensed milk mixture into the cream that has been whipped. This is your ice cream base. You will want this to be as smooth as possible and lump free.

Pour half of the ice cream base into an 8 x 8–inch (20 x 20–cm) baking pan (or a freezer-safe container of about the same size), and using your spatula, spread the ice cream evenly throughout the pan. Using half of the prepared and cooled caramel, spoon large tablespoons (15 ml) over the ice cream base. Pour the remaining half of the ice cream base into the pan, and finally, drizzle the remaining caramel over the ice cream base. Using a butter knife or fork, gently swirl the caramel into the base, ensuring that you do not overmix it. You'll want those delightful pockets of caramel to be present throughout the ice cream. Freeze the ice cream uncovered for 3 to 5 hours or overnight, until it is firm. Cover any leftovers with tinfoil or plastic wrap, and store them in the freezer for up to 3 weeks.

VARIATION: *How about a chocolate caramel cheesecake ripple? Add a ½ cup (50 g) of unsweetened Dutch-processed cocoa powder to the sweetened condensed milk and cream mixture before folding in the whipped cream. Continue as instructed.*

For the Ice Cream

4 oz (113 g) cream cheese, softened to room temperature

1 (14-oz [414-ml]) can sweetened condensed milk

½ cup (120 ml) half-and-half

2 tsp (10 ml) pure vanilla extract

1½ cups (360 ml) heavy cream

PUMPKIN CHEESECAKE

This recipe yields roughly 12–14 standard scoops.

4 oz (113 g) cream cheese, softened to room temperature

1 (14-oz [414-ml]) can sweetened condensed milk

½ cup (120 ml) half-and-half

2 tsp (10 ml) pure vanilla extract

½ cup (73 g) pumpkin purée

½ tsp ground cinnamon

¼ tsp ground nutmeg

⅛ tsp ground cloves

1½ cups (360 ml) heavy cream

The flavors of pumpkin permeate autumn each and every year. When the pumpkins come out, bakers around the globe begin concocting tantalizing treats to utilize this incredible vegetable. One of my favorite desserts is pumpkin cheesecake, and I wanted to bring those flavors to life in a no-churn ice cream form.

Classic pumpkin pie spices, cinnamon, nutmeg and cloves are added to this base for an incredible pop of true pumpkin pie flavor. When combined with the creaminess and tartness of cream cheese, the pumpkin cheesecake flavor is undeniable.

If you wanted to up the ante even further, you could bake up a batch of shortbread cookies and serve scoops of ice cream on them for even more fall flavor.

In a medium-sized bowl, whisk the softened cream cheese until it is light and fluffy, for about 1 minute. Add in the sweetened condensed milk and half-and-half, and whisk until combined. Add the pure vanilla extract, pumpkin purée, cinnamon, nutmeg and cloves. Whisk everything together, until the mixture is smooth. Set this aside. With a standing or hand mixer, whip the heavy cream until stiff peaks form, 60 to 90 seconds. Fold the sweetened condensed milk mixture into the cream that has been whipped. This is your ice cream base. You will want this to be as smooth as possible and lump free.

Pour the ice cream into an 8 x 8-inch (20 x 20–cm) baking pan (or a freezer-safe container of about the same size), and using your spatula, spread the ice cream evenly throughout the pan. Freeze the ice cream uncovered for 3 to 5 hours or overnight, until it is firm. Cover any leftovers with tinfoil or plastic wrap, and store them in the freezer for up to 3 weeks.

VARIATION: *Pumpkin caramel cheesecake would be a divine flavor, so to make this, simply swirl in caramel from page 75 before freezing as instructed. Want to take it up another notch? Make the shortbread from the Blueberry Pie recipe (page 117) and crumble that into this recipe for a full-on pumpkin pie or pumpkin caramel pie experience.*

Carnival Inspired

Warm summer nights and endless rides . . . bright neon lights and concerts under the stars . . . many of these images might come to mind when recounting days spent at a local carnival. The number one thing we recall though, is definitely the array of goodies. Fluffy, hand-spun cotton candy, ice-cold lemonade, mouthwatering caramel popcorn and homemade award-winning blueberry pie are among the memories we can't shake, and thus they became staples for this chapter. Inspired by our favorite fair time treats, welcome to the carnival-inspired chapter.

COTTON CANDY

This recipe yields roughly 12–14 standard scoops.

1 (14-oz [414-ml]) can sweetened condensed milk

1 tbsp (15 ml) cotton candy flavoring

½ cup (120 ml) half-and-half

1½ cups (360 ml) heavy cream

Pink and blue food coloring (optional)

While this particular ice cream uses no actual cotton candy (spun sugar does not do well in cold temperatures!), I use cotton candy flavoring and bright colors to create the flavor and visual appeal of real cotton candy. The unique flavor of cotton candy is paired with the lusciously creamy no-churn ice cream base.

Add a small fluff of actual cotton candy to a scoop of this pretty ice cream immediately before serving it for a little extra flair.

In a medium-sized bowl, whisk together the sweetened condensed milk, cotton candy flavoring and half-and-half, until the mixture is smooth. Set this aside. With a standing or hand mixer, whip the heavy cream until stiff peaks form, 60 to 90 seconds. Fold the sweetened condensed milk mixture into the cream that has been whipped. This is your ice cream base. You will want this to be as smooth as possible and lump free.

If you are using the food coloring, divide the ice cream base evenly between two small bowls. Use 3 to 5 drops of blue food coloring in one bowl, and 3 to 5 drops of pink food coloring in the other bowl. Add additional food coloring to each bowl if you desire the color to be darker. Gently fold the food coloring into each bowl with a spatula (using two spatulas or washing the one before using it in the second bowl) until the color is evenly distributed throughout the bowls.

Pour the ice cream into an 8 x 8–inch (20 x 20–cm) baking pan (or a freezer-safe container of about the same size), and using your spatula, spread the ice cream evenly throughout the pan. Carefully swirl the pink and blue bases together in the pan, making sure to keep them distinct. Freeze the ice cream uncovered for 3 to 5 hours or overnight, until it is firm. Cover any leftovers with tinfoil or plastic wrap, and store them in the freezer for up to 3 weeks.

VARIATION: *If you'd like to flavor your cotton candy with fruit, you can add 1 teaspoon of strawberry or raspberry extract when you add in the cotton candy flavoring. Continue as instructed.*

CARAMEL APPLE SWIRL

This recipe yields roughly 12–14 standard scoops.

Caramel apples might be one of the most iconic treats in the history of carnival attendance. A delightfully tart apple is coated with a sweet and salty + buttery caramel sauce, and sometimes even dipped in a candy coating for that extra little bit of goodness.

This no-churn ice cream copies the appeal by using chunks of real apples that have been cooked until just soft. Swirls of homemade caramel and pure vanilla extract mimic the delightful carnival treat that so many know and love.

For the Caramel
½ cup (100 g) granulated sugar

¼ cup (57 g) salted butter

¼ cup (60 ml) heavy cream

To make the caramel, begin by placing the granulated sugar in a small saucepan on the stovetop, over medium to high heat. Whisk the sugar continuously without stopping until it is melted. Be very cautious, as you do not want the sugar to burn, and be aware of splatter. It will be extremely hot!

Once the sugar reduces to a dark amber-colored liquid, about 3 to 5 minutes, add the butter. Whisk this bubbly liquid until it is fully combined and no lumps remain. Lower the heat to a simmer. Slowly add the heavy cream and mix the caramel, until it is well combined. Remove the pan from the heat and allow the caramel to cool completely. The caramel will thicken as it cools. If your mixture clumps up at all, simply pop the pan back onto the burner and then turn the heat up to medium for 1 or 2 minutes of vigorous stirring. It will come together.

You can place the pan in the refrigerator to speed up the cooling process. I generally allow my caramel to cool for 45 to 60 minutes. You will use all of this caramel in this recipe, but should you choose to double it and have some extra, you can store any leftovers in an airtight glass container for up to 1 month in the refrigerator. You can warm the caramel to loosen it up after it has been refrigerated, as it will stiffen. It is still pliable though, so it can be eaten warm or cold.

Make the apples before putting the ice cream base together so they have plenty of time to cool.

(continued)

CARAMEL APPLE SWIRL (cont.)

For the Ice Cream

4 medium-sized apples (any variety will do, so pick your favorite!)

1 (14-oz [414-ml]) can sweetened condensed milk

1 tbsp (15 ml) pure vanilla extract

½ cup (120 ml) half-and-half

1½ cups (360 ml) heavy cream

Peel, core and slice each apple into 1-inch (2.5-cm) cubes. Place the apples in a medium-sized saucepan and fill the pan with enough water to cover the apples. Place on the stovetop over medium high heat. Once the water comes to a boil, cook the fruit for 10 minutes. Keep an eye on the pan so that the water does not overflow. If the bubbles get too close to the top, reduce the heat to medium. When the time is up, strain the apples and place them in a bowl in the refrigerator to cool completely.

In a medium-sized bowl, whisk together the sweetened condensed milk, pure vanilla extract and half-and-half, until the mixture is smooth. Set this aside. With a standing or hand mixer, whip the heavy cream until stiff peaks form, 60 to 90 seconds. Fold the sweetened condensed milk mixture into the cream that has been whipped. This is your ice cream base. You will want this to be as smooth as possible and lump free. Remove the chilled apples from the refrigerator and fold them into the ice cream base, ensuring that you distribute the apples as evenly as possible.

Pour half of the ice cream base into an 8 x 8–inch (20 x 20–cm) baking pan (or a freezer-safe container of about the same size), and using your spatula, spread the ice cream evenly throughout the pan. Using half of the prepared and cooled caramel, spoon large tablespoons (15 ml) over the ice cream base. Pour the remaining half of the ice cream base into the pan, and finally, drizzle the remaining caramel over the ice cream base. Using a butter knife or fork, gently swirl the caramel into the base, ensuring that you do not overmix it. You'll want those delightful pockets of caramel to be present throughout the ice cream. Freeze the ice cream uncovered for 3 to 5 hours or overnight, until it is firm. Cover any leftovers with tinfoil or plastic wrap, and store them in the freezer for up to 3 weeks.

VARIATION: *Caramel pears have gained momentum in recent years, so switch out apples for pears at a one-to-one ratio in this recipe if you love that combination.*

PEACH CRUMBLE

This recipe yields roughly 12–14 standard scoops.

Peaches are one of the oldest stone fruits to have ever been cultivated around the world. Their sweet flavor tantalizes the senses, while the soft texture is downright euphoric.

This peach crumble ice cream uses fresh ripe peaches that have been softened ever so slightly by cooking them on the stovetop. A delightful crumble is baked to golden perfection, and both the crumble and the peaches are added to a scrumptious cinnamon vanilla ice cream base.

You will want to make the crumble and cook the peaches first, so they both have plenty of time to cool down before adding them to the ice cream base.

To make the crumble, begin by preheating the oven to 350°F (177°C).

In a small bowl, whisk together the dark brown sugar, flour, oats, ground cinnamon, nutmeg and cloves. Add the salted butter, and using a fork, gently combine until a crumbly mixture forms. Line a small baking sheet with parchment paper. Pour the crumble mixture onto the parchment paper, and spread out evenly to about ½ inch (1.3 cm) thick. Bake the crumble for 10 to 15 minutes, or until golden-brown. Remove the crumble from the oven and allow it to cool completely before breaking into pieces.

While the crumble is baking, make your peaches. Peel, core and slice your peaches into 1-inch (2.5-cm) cubes. Place the peaches in a medium-sized saucepan and add enough water to cover them. Place the saucepan on the stovetop over medium to high heat. Once the water begins to boil, cook for 5 to 10 minutes, or until the peaches are slightly soft to the touch. Be cautious that the water does not bubble over and also be careful of splatter, as it could be hot.

Remove the peaches from the heat, strain and pour them into a bowl. Place the bowl in the refrigerator so the peaches can cool down completely before adding them to the ice cream base.

(continued)

For the Crumble

½ cup (110 g) firmly packed dark brown sugar

⅓ cup (43 g) all-purpose flour

½ cup (40 g) old fashioned or quick oats

1 tsp ground cinnamon

½ tsp ground nutmeg

¼ tsp ground cloves

¼ cup (57 g) salted butter, softened

For the Ice Cream

4 medium-sized, ripe peaches

1 (14-oz [414-ml]) can sweetened condensed milk

2 tsp (10 ml) pure vanilla extract

2 tsp (5 g) ground cinnamon

½ cup (120 ml) half-and-half

1½ cups (360 ml) heavy cream

PEACH CRUMBLE (cont.)

In a medium-sized bowl, make the ice cream by whisking together the sweetened condensed milk, pure vanilla extract, ground cinnamon and half-and-half, until the mixture is smooth. Set this aside. With a standing or hand mixer, whip the heavy cream until stiff peaks form, 60 to 90 seconds. Fold the sweetened condensed milk mixture into the cream that has been whipped. This is your ice cream base. You will want this to be as smooth as possible and lump free.

Add the cold peaches and the pieces of crumble to the ice cream base. Gently fold them in, ensuring that the peaches and the crumble are well dispersed throughout the ice cream base.

Pour the ice cream into an 8 x 8–inch (20 x 20–cm) baking pan (or a freezer-safe container of about the same size), and using your spatula, spread the ice cream evenly throughout the pan. Freeze the ice cream uncovered for 3 to 5 hours or overnight, until it is firm. Cover any leftovers with tinfoil or plastic wrap, and store them in the freezer for up to 3 weeks.

VARIATION: *You can substitute with apples for a fun fall-inspired ice cream! Apple crisp is a super popular dessert, so simply substitute with apples for peaches and make as instructed.*

BLACKBERRY LEMONADE

This recipe yields roughly 12–14 standard scoops.

Blackberry lemonade is summertime joy, especially on a sun-drenched day. Whether riding carnival rides all day or walking the dusty grounds of a fair to see all that there is to see, nothing quenches thirst quite like a tall glass of ice-cold lemonade.

This blackberry lemonade no-churn ice cream uses the same fresh blackberry sauce that I used in my Blackberry Cheesecake (page 93). It also uses pure lemon extract in the base for that perfect tart kick of lemony goodness.

To make the blackberry sauce, place the blackberries, granulated sugar, cornstarch and fresh lemon juice in a medium-sized saucepan. Place the pan on the stovetop over medium-high heat. Using a potato masher, begin to mash the fruit and ingredients, until they come together as the mixture starts to warm up. After 1 to 2 minutes of cooking, the mixture will begin to bubble. Lower the heat to medium, and stir frequently until the fruit sauce thickens, another 1 to 2 minutes. Remove the mixture from the heat, and transfer to a bowl. Refrigerate until completely cool, about 30 minutes.

In a medium-sized bowl, make the ice cream by whisking together the sweetened condensed milk, pure vanilla extract, pure lemon extract and half-and-half, until it is smooth. Set this aside. With a standing or hand mixer, whip the heavy cream until stiff peaks form, 60 to 90 seconds. Fold the sweetened condensed milk mixture into the cream that has been whipped. This is your ice cream base. You will want this to be as smooth as possible and lump free.

Pour the ice cream into an 8 x 8-inch (20 x 20-cm) baking pan (or a freezer-safe container of about the same size), and using your spatula, spread the ice cream evenly throughout the pan. Remove the blackberry sauce mixture from the refrigerator. Using a tablespoon, drop the mixture all over the top of the ice cream base, using all of it up. Take a butter knife or fork, and swirl the mixture into the base, ensuring that it is dispersed throughout the ice cream. Freeze the ice cream uncovered for 3 to 5 hours or overnight, until it is firm. Cover any leftovers with tinfoil or plastic wrap, and store them in the freezer for up to 3 weeks.

For the Blackberry Sauce

2 cups (246 g) fresh blackberries

½ cup (100 g) granulated sugar

2 tbsp (16 g) cornstarch

2 tbsp (30 ml) fresh squeezed lemon juice

For the Ice Cream

1 (14-oz [414-ml]) can sweetened condensed milk

2 tsp (10 ml) pure vanilla extract

1 tbsp (15 ml) pure lemon extract

½ cup (120 ml) half-and-half

1½ cups (360 ml) heavy cream

VARIATION: *Choose your favorite berry for this recipe! For example, if you love strawberries or raspberries, substitute either of those berries for the blackberries and make the rest as instructed.*

CARAMEL POPCORN CRUNCH

This recipe yields roughly 12–14 standard scoops.

For the Caramel

½ cup (100 g) granulated sugar

¼ cup (57 g) salted butter

¼ cup (60 ml) heavy cream

The intoxicating scent of freshly made warm caramel popcorn is undeniable. This incredibly easy and sweet + buttery caramel popcorn crunch ice cream begins with my vanilla base. I add my signature homemade caramel sauce in generous swirls throughout, and plenty of sweet and salty caramel popcorn. The result is a tantalizing and satisfying frozen popcorn treat that is as delicious as it is unique.

To make the caramel, begin by placing the granulated sugar in a small saucepan on the stovetop, over medium to high heat. Whisk the sugar continuously without stopping until it is melted. Be very cautious, as you do not want the sugar to burn, and be aware of splatter. It will be extremely hot!

Once the sugar reduces to a dark amber-colored liquid, about 3 to 5 minutes, add the butter. Whisk this bubbly liquid until it is fully combined, and no lumps remain. Lower the heat to a simmer. Slowly add the heavy cream and mix the caramel, until it is well combined. Remove the pan from the heat and allow the caramel to cool completely. The caramel will thicken as it cools. If your mixture clumps up at all, simply pop the pan back onto the burner and then turn the heat up to medium for a minute or two of vigorous stirring. It will come together.

You can place the pan in the refrigerator to speed up the cooling process. I generally allow my caramel to cool for 45 to 60 minutes. You will use all of this caramel in this recipe, but should you choose to double it and have some extra, you can store any leftovers in an airtight glass container for up to 1 month in the refrigerator. You can warm up the caramel to loosen it up after it has been refrigerated, as it will stiffen. It is still pliable though, so it can be eaten warm or cold.

(continued)

For the Ice Cream

1 (14-oz [414-ml]) can sweetened condensed milk

2 tsp (10 ml) pure vanilla extract

½ cup (120 ml) half-and-half

1½ cups (360 ml) heavy cream

1½ cups (65 g) caramel popcorn of choice

In a medium-sized bowl, make the ice cream by whisking together the sweetened condensed milk, pure vanilla extract and half-and-half, until the mixture is smooth. Set this aside. With a standing or hand mixer, whip the heavy cream until stiff peaks form, 60 to 90 seconds. Fold the sweetened condensed milk mixture into the cream that has been whipped. This is your ice cream base. You will want this to be as smooth as possible and lump free. Add the caramel popcorn, and gently fold it in with a spatula. You want to ensure that it is evenly distributed throughout the ice cream base.

Pour half of the ice cream base into an 8 x 8–inch (20 x 20–cm) baking pan (or a freezer-safe container of about the same size), and using your spatula, spread the ice cream evenly throughout the pan. Using half of the prepared and cooled caramel, spoon large tablespoons (15 ml) over the ice cream base. Pour the remaining half of the ice cream base into the pan, and finally, drizzle the remaining caramel over the ice cream base. Using a butter knife or fork, gently swirl the caramel into the base, ensuring that you do not over mix it. You'll want those delightful pockets of caramel to be present throughout the ice cream. Freeze the ice cream uncovered for 3 to 5 hours or overnight, until it is firm. Cover any leftovers with tinfoil or plastic wrap, and store them in the freezer for up to 3 weeks.

VARIATION: *Use chocolate-covered popcorn clusters for an even more decadent combination! Also, you could run a fudge ripple right through this base and it would be excellent as well. Use the recipe from page 56.*

BLUEBERRY PIE

This recipe yields roughly 12–14 standard scoops.

Blueberry pie bake-offs and summer fairs practically go hand-in-hand. A gloriously buttery pie crust nestles fresh blueberries, vanilla and sugar inside. It's tart and sweet and oh-so-satisfying. This no-churn ice cream version uses fresh blueberries and a baked shortbread cookie to mimic the crust of real pie. It's truly a lovely combination that can be enjoyed any time of the year.

Preheat oven to 350°F (177°C). Using either a standing or hand mixer, or a plastic or wooden spoon, mix together the butter, both sugars, egg yolk and pure vanilla extract, until smooth. Add in the flour and baking powder, and mix well. The dough should be soft and moldable but not sticky. There is no need to chill this dough.

Roll the dough out to about ¼ inch (6 mm) thick. Use a 1-inch (2.5-cm) square cookie cutter if you have one. If not, use any cookie cutter that you have on hand. You can simply break up larger cookies into smaller chunks to add to the ice cream base. Using up all the dough, cut cookies out and place them on a baking sheet about 2 inches (5 cm) apart. These cookies will not spread in the oven. Bake for 6 to 8 minutes or until they are ever so slightly golden on the edges, being cautious not to over-bake them. Remove the cookies from the oven and allow them to cool for 1 minute on the baking sheet. Remove them from the baking sheet and allow them to cool completely on a baking rack.

(continued)

For the Shortbread

½ cup (114 g) salted butter, softened

¼ cup (50 g) granulated sugar

¼ cup (55 g) firmly packed brown sugar

1 large egg yolk

1 tsp pure vanilla extract

1¼ cups (160 g) all-purpose flour

1 tsp baking powder

BLUEBERRY PIE (cont.)

In a medium-sized bowl, make the ice cream by whisking together the sweetened condensed milk, pure vanilla extract and half-and-half, until it is smooth. Set this aside. With a standing or hand mixer, whip the heavy cream until stiff peaks form, 60 to 90 seconds. Fold the sweetened condensed milk mixture into the cream that has been whipped. This is your ice cream base. You will want this to be as smooth as possible and lump free. Add in the fresh blueberries and the 1-inch (2.5-cm) cookie pieces or broken cookie chunks to the ice cream base, and fold everything in gently. Ensure that they are both evenly distributed throughout the ice cream.

Pour the ice cream into an 8 x 8–inch (20 x 20–cm) baking pan (or a freezer-safe container of about the same size), and using your spatula, spread the ice cream evenly throughout the pan. Freeze the ice cream uncovered for 3 to 5 hours or overnight, until it is firm. Cover any left-overs with tinfoil or plastic wrap, and store them in the freezer for up to 3 weeks.

VARIATION: *You can substitute your favorite berry for this pie-inspired ice cream recipe. Simply choose your berry and make as instructed.*

For the Ice Cream

1 (14-oz [414-ml]) can sweetened condensed milk

1 tbsp (15 ml) pure vanilla extract

½ cup (120 ml) half-and-half

1½ cups (360 ml) heavy cream

2 cups (296 g) fresh blueberries

Bars + Sandwiches

This final chapter brings some special extras to life that I just couldn't leave out. Cookies and ice cream belong together, so included in this last section are some of my favorite ice cream cookie sandwiches. From peanut butter to caramel to mint to so much dark chocolate, there's a little something for every taste in extra indulgence.

Ice cream bars are super fun, and although I think it's great to have a mold of your own, the lack of owning one shouldn't keep you from creating any of these bars. In lieu of filling ice cream molds to make the bars, you will simply line a 9 x 13-inch (23 x 33-cm) baking dish with parchment paper (ensuring that you leave a little hanging over the edge so you can remove it as one unit), pour the frozen ice cream into the dish and freeze from there. Once the ice cream is set, you will remove the ice cream by lifting the parchment paper. Cut the ice cream into equal rectangles, push the sticks through the ends of the rectangles and dip each one into the chocolate, and refreeze them in the same way as if they came out of the mold. Work in small batches here too, as you don't want the ice cream to melt as you go.

MILK CHOCOLATE–DIPPED VANILLA ICE CREAM BARS

This recipe yields 14–16 ice cream bars.

For the Ice Cream

1 (14-oz [414-g]) can sweetened condensed milk

1 tbsp (15 ml) pure vanilla extract

½ cup (120 ml) half-and-half

1½ cups (360 ml) heavy cream

For the Chocolate Dip

1½ cups (248 g) milk chocolate chips

2 tbsp (30 ml) coconut oil

VARIATION: *You can use ANY ice cream flavor from this book— mold it and dip it in chocolate!*

These ice cream bars are reminiscent of the classic Magnum® bars that you can still find in stores. Homemade vanilla ice cream is dipped in delicious milk chocolate and enjoyed right off the stick!

If you do not have an ice cream mold you can use a parchment paper–lined 9 x 13–inch (23 x 33–cm) baking dish, see page 121.

In a medium-sized bowl, make the ice cream by whisking together the sweetened condensed milk, pure vanilla extract and half-and-half, until the mixture is smooth. Set this aside. With a standing or hand mixer, whip the heavy cream until stiff peaks form, 60 to 90 seconds. Gently fold the sweetened condensed milk mixture into the cream that has been whipped. You will want this to be as smooth as possible and lump free.

Fill each mold with the vanilla ice cream base and insert wooden sticks. Freeze the ice cream bars uncovered for 3 to 5 hours or overnight. They should be completely solid before you dip them in the chocolate.

To make the chocolate dip, combine the chocolate chips and coconut oil in a small microwave-safe bowl. Microwave on high for 30 seconds, and then remove the bowl and give the mixture a good stir. Keep heating the mixture in additional 30-second increments until it is completely smooth and lump free. Be cautious, as the bowl and the mixture could get hot. Pour the melted chocolate mixture into any tall skinny glass that fits the ice cream bars so they can be fully submerged in the chocolate.

Unmold the vanilla ice cream bars, working in batches of one to two bars at a time. Keep the other ice cream bars frozen while you work so that they do not melt before they are dipped. Dip each vanilla ice cream bar in the melted chocolate, and then place them on a sheet of parchment paper. The chocolate should harden within 30 seconds. Place the ice cream bars back in the freezer for an additional hour, or you may consume them right away, if desired. Store any leftovers in a covered freezer-safe container for up to 2 weeks.

STRAWBERRY CHEESECAKE ICE CREAM BARS

This recipe yields 14–16 ice cream bars.

The sweetness of strawberries meets the elegance of vanilla cheesecake in these perfect-for-summer strawberry cheesecake ice cream bars. If you do not have an ice cream mold and still want to make these, you can substitute the ice cream mold with a parchment paper–lined 9 x 13–inch (23 x 33–cm) baking dish. Simply follow the instructions in the chapter intro for this method (page 121).

4 oz (113 g) cream cheese, softened to room temperature

1 (14-oz [414-ml]) can sweetened condensed milk

½ cup (120 ml) half-and-half

1 tbsp (15 ml) pure vanilla extract

1½ cups (360 ml) heavy cream

30 medium-sized fresh strawberries, hulled and chopped

In a medium-sized bowl, whisk the softened cream cheese until it is light and fluffy, for about 1 minute. Add the sweetened condensed milk, half-and-half and vanilla extract. Whisk until combined. Set this aside. With a standing or hand mixer, whip the heavy cream until stiff peaks form, 60 to 90 seconds. Fold the sweetened condensed milk mixture into the cream that has been whipped. This is your ice cream base. You will want this to be as smooth as possible and lump free. Fold the strawberries into the cheesecake base.

Fill each mold with the strawberry cheesecake ice cream base and insert wooden sticks. Freeze the ice cream bars uncovered for 3 to 5 hours or overnight. They should be completely solid before serving.

Unmold the ice cream bars and serve right away. Store any leftovers in the freezer in a covered freezer-safe container for up to 2 weeks.

VARIATION: *Use your favorite berry in place of strawberries and make as instructed. This would make an excellent ice cream sandwich as well, sandwiched between graham crackers for a full strawberry cheesecake experience.*

DOUBLE DARK CHOCOLATE CHIP ICE CREAM BARS

This recipe yields 14–16 ice cream bars.

For the Ice Cream

1 (14-oz [414-ml]) can sweetened condensed milk

1 tbsp (15 ml) pure vanilla extract

½ cup (120 ml) half-and-half

½ cup (50 g) dark cocoa powder

1½ cups (248 g) dark chocolate chips

1½ cups (360 ml) heavy cream

For these delicious dark chocolate bars, I take my milk chocolate–dipped vanilla ice cream bars and up the chocolate-ante like you wouldn't believe. Dark chocolate ice cream is blended with dark chocolate chips and dipped in a glorious dark chocolate coating. It's a dark chocolate lover's dream, and it's easy to boot.

If you do not have an ice cream mold and still want to make these, you can substitute the ice cream mold with a parchment paper–lined 9 x 13–inch (23 x 33–cm) baking dish. Simply follow the instructions in the chapter intro for this method (page 121).

In a medium-sized bowl, make the ice cream by whisking together the sweetened condensed milk, pure vanilla extract and half-and-half, until the mixture is smooth. Stir in the dark cocoa powder until no loose powder remains. Gently stir in the dark chocolate chips, ensuring that there is an even distribution throughout the mixture. Set this aside.

With a standing or hand mixer, whip the heavy cream until stiff peaks form, 60 to 90 seconds. Fold the sweetened condensed milk mixture into the cream that has been whipped. This is your ice cream base. You will want this to be as smooth as possible and lump free.

Fill each mold with the dark chocolate ice cream base and insert wooden sticks. Freeze the ice cream bars uncovered for 3 to 5 hours or overnight. They should be completely solid before serving. Unmold the ice cream bars and serve right away. Store any leftovers in the freezer in a covered freezer-safe container for up to 2 weeks.

VARIATION: *Substitute with your favorite chips (milk, white or semi-sweet would work in place of dark) and swirl in some caramel from page 75 for an ooey-gooey treat. Dip it in chocolate from page 122 if you want to be totally extra in the best way possible.*

CARAMEL PEANUT CRUNCH ICE CREAM BARS

This recipe yields 14–16 ice cream bars.

Peanuts and caramel are about the sweetest, saltiest, most buttery combination that you can find. These caramel peanut crunch ice cream bars begin with a glorious caramel no-churn ice cream base. More caramel is swirled throughout the mixture, and crunchy salty peanuts are mixed right in. They are deceptively easy. If you do not have an ice cream mold and still want to make these, you can substitute the ice cream mold with a parchment paper–lined 9 x 13–inch (23 x 33–cm) baking dish. Simply follow the instructions in the chapter intro for this method (page 121).

For the Caramel

½ cup (100 g) granulated sugar

¼ cup (57 g) salted butter

¼ cup (60 ml) heavy cream

To make the caramel, place the granulated sugar in a small saucepan on the stovetop, over medium to high heat. Whisk the sugar continuously without stopping until it is melted. Be very cautious, as you do not want the sugar to burn, and be aware of splatter. It will be extremely hot!

Once the sugar reduces to a dark amber-colored liquid, about 3 to 5 minutes, add the butter. Whisk this bubbly liquid until it is fully combined, and no lumps remain. Lower the heat to a simmer.

Slowly add the heavy cream and mix the caramel, until it is well combined. Remove the pan from the heat and allow the caramel to cool completely. The caramel will thicken as it cools. If your mixture clumps up at all, simply pop the pan back onto the burner and then turn the heat up to medium for 1 or 2 minutes of vigorous stirring. It will come together.

You can place the pan in the refrigerator to speed up the cooling process. I generally allow my caramel to cool for 45 to 60 minutes. You will use all of this caramel in this recipe, but should you choose to double it and have some extra, you can store any leftovers in an airtight glass container for up to 1 month in the refrigerator. You can warm the caramel to loosen it up after it has been refrigerated, as it will stiffen. It is still pliable though, so it can be eaten warm or cold.

(continued)

CARAMEL PEANUT CRUNCH ICE CREAM BARS (CONT.)

For the Ice Cream

1 (14-oz can [414-ml]) sweetened condensed milk

2 tsp (10 ml) pure vanilla extract

½ cup (120 ml) half-and-half

1½ cups (360 ml) heavy cream

1 cup (146 g) salted peanuts, chopped

In a medium-sized bowl, make the ice cream by whisking together the sweetened condensed milk, half of the cooled caramel sauce, pure vanilla extract and half-and-half, until it is smooth. Set this aside. With a standing or hand mixer, whip the heavy cream until stiff peaks form, 60 to 90 seconds. Fold the sweetened condensed milk mixture into the cream that has been whipped. This is your ice cream base. You will want this to be as smooth as possible and lump free. Fold the salted peanuts in, ensuring that you evenly distribute them throughout the ice cream base. By tablespoons (15 ml), drop the remaining half of the caramel sauce around the ice cream, gently swirling it in with a butter knife or fork. Do not overmix, as you want those tasty pockets of caramel to be ever present in these ice cream bars!

Fill each mold with the caramel peanut ice cream base and insert wooden sticks. Freeze the ice cream bars uncovered for 3 to 5 hours or overnight. They should be completely solid before serving. Add some extra caramel drizzle and chopped peanuts to the top if you want to enjoy extra gooeyness with these fabulous bars.

Unmold the ice cream bars and serve right away. Store any leftovers in the freezer in a covered freezer-safe container for up to 2 weeks.

VARIATION: *If you love chocolate and wish to incorporate it here, you could get super creative. Mix in a ½ cup (83 g) of your favorite chocolate chips, dip the bar in the chocolate from page 122 or go totally nutty and do both. You get extra points for both.*

PEANUT BUTTER PARTY COOKIE SANDWICHES

This recipe yields 10–12 ice cream cookie sandwiches.

We have officially moved onto the last portion of this book, and since cookies are my favorite food in the entire universe, it is officially the best part of the book (in my humble opinion). Enter: The ice cream cookie sandwiches. I begin this section with a peanut butter explosion. Soft and flavorful peanut butter cookies are sandwiched around luscious peanut butter no-churn ice cream.

Now if you cannot have peanut butter, or you prefer almond butter, you can substitute almond butter for peanut butter at a one-to-one ratio in both the cookies and the ice cream.

For the Ice Cream

1 (14-oz [414-ml]) can sweetened condensed milk

½ cup (129 g) all-natural, no-sugar-added peanut butter (I use Adams salted peanut butter)

2 tsp (10 ml) pure vanilla extract

½ cup (120 g) half-and-half

1½ cups (360 ml) heavy cream

It is best to make the ice cream first, as it needs several hours (or overnight!) to become solid. Baking and freezing the cookies is step two, but by all means, reverse the steps if you'd like to enjoy some fresh baked cookies before or while you make the ice cream!

Prepare two 8-inch (20-cm) round or square pans by lining them with parchment paper. Ensure that the parchment has a bit of overhang so that you can remove the ice cream as a whole unit once it is fully frozen.

In a medium-sized bowl, make the ice cream by whisking together the sweetened condensed milk, all-natural peanut butter, pure vanilla extract and half-and-half, until the mixture is smooth. Set this aside. With a standing or hand mixer, whip the heavy cream until stiff peaks form, 60 to 90 seconds. Gently fold the sweetened condensed milk mixture into the cream that has been whipped. You will want this to be as smooth as possible and lump free.

Separate the ice cream into your two parchment-lined pans. Using a spatula, spread the ice cream evenly throughout the pans. You will want the ice cream to be ½ to ¾ inch (1.3 to 2 cm) thick for an optimum ratio when sandwiched between the cookies. Cover the ice cream pans with tinfoil or plastic wrap, and freeze them uncovered for 3 to 5 hours or overnight, until firm.

(continued)

For the Cookies

½ cup (114 g) salted butter, softened

½ cup (110 g) firmly packed dark brown sugar

¼ cup (50 g) granulated sugar

1 large egg

½ tsp baking soda

½ tsp salt

1 tsp pure vanilla extract

1¼ cups (160 g) all-purpose flour

To make the cookies, begin by preheating the oven to 375°F (190°C). Cream the butter in a standing mixer or with a hand mixer for about 30 seconds, and then add both of the sugars. Continue to cream until light and fluffy, about 30 seconds. Add the egg. Mix until well incorporated, and then add the baking soda, salt and vanilla. Give it another good mix, and then add the flour. Mix until the dough is formed, about 30 seconds.

Using a 2-teaspoon (10-ml) cookie scoop to make balls, spoon the balls onto a nonstick baking sheet and gently press down with a potato masher or fork. Bake the cookies for 8 to 10 minutes, or until golden on the edges. Cool the cookies on the cookie sheet for 5 minutes, and then transfer them to a baking rack to cool completely. Place the cookies in the freezer for 1 hour to harden them up. This will allow the cookie sandwiches to come together and stay frozen when assembling.

It is best to work in batches so that both the ice cream and the cookies remain fully frozen. Remove six cookies and one pan of ice cream at a time. Using a 3- or 4-inch (8- or 10-cm) round cookie or biscuit cutter, cut circles into the ice cream and place each ice cream "disk" between two frozen cookies. Gently press down and refreeze the cookie sandwiches until you are ready to consume them. Repeat this process with the second pan of ice cream and the remaining six cookies. You may want to refreeze the ice cream for a short period of time if you find that it is becoming soft as you assemble the sandwiches.

Store any leftover cookies in a covered container in the freezer for up to 2 weeks.

VARIATION: *You could absolutely swirl in the peanut butter swirl from page 49 to the ice cream base, or even add a ½ cup (125 g) of crushed peanut butter cups. Or both. And then we'd need to rename these the "ultimate supreme peanut butter party cookies". It has a nice ring.*

DOUBLE MINT CHOCOLATE COOKIE SANDWICHES

This recipe yields 12–14 ice cream cookie sandwiches.

If you like chocolate peppermint, this glorious shortbread cookie with mint chocolate chip ice cream in the center is sure to make your day. I use pure peppermint extract to bring out an authentic mint flavor. Dark chocolate chips are folded into the dark mint chocolate ice cream, and the combination is so decadent.

Mix it up: If you love dark chocolate but mint isn't your thing, simply omit the peppermint extract from both recipes and replace it with more pure vanilla extract.

It is best to make the ice cream first, as it needs several hours (or overnight!) to become solid. Baking and freezing the cookies is step two, but by all means, reverse the steps if you'd like to enjoy some fresh baked cookies before or while you make the ice cream!

Prepare two 8-inch (20-cm) round or square pans by lining them with parchment paper. Ensure that the parchment has a bit of overhang so that you can remove the ice cream as a whole unit once it is fully frozen.

In a medium-sized bowl, make the ice cream by whisking together the sweetened condensed milk, pure vanilla extract, pure peppermint extract and half-and-half until the mixture is smooth. Stir in the dark cocoa powder until no loose powder remains. Set this aside. With a standing or hand mixer, whip the heavy cream until stiff peaks form, 60 to 90 seconds. Fold the sweetened condensed milk mixture into the cream that has been whipped. This is your ice cream base. You will want this to be as smooth as possible and lump free. Fold in the dark chocolate chips, ensuring that they are evenly distributed throughout the ice cream base.

For the Ice Cream

1 (14-oz [414-ml]) can sweetened condensed milk

2 tsp (10 ml) pure vanilla extract

2 tsp (10 ml) pure peppermint extract

½ cup (120 ml) half-and-half

½ cup (50 g) dark cocoa powder

1½ cups (360 ml) heavy cream

1½ cups (248 g) dark chocolate chips

(continued)

For the Cookies

½ cup (113 g) salted butter, softened

¼ cup (55 g) firmly packed dark brown sugar

¼ cup (50 g) granulated sugar

1 tsp pure vanilla extract

1 tsp pure peppermint extract

1 large egg yolk

1 tsp baking soda

¼ cup (25 g) dark cocoa powder

1¼ cups (156 g) all-purpose flour

VARIATION: *Love chocolate but not totally sold on mint? Omit it. Enjoy the chocolate and nothing else. You could also sub any flavor of ice cream in this book that you'd like to try between these shortbread cookies. You can also make the vanilla shortbread cookies from the Blueberry Pie ice cream recipe on page 117 and turn those into any flavor combo of sandwich cookie with any ice cream flavor in this book. Go ahead, experiment away. I wholeheartedly approve.*

Separate the ice cream into your two parchment-lined pans. Using a spatula, spread the ice cream evenly throughout the pans. You will want the ice cream to be ½ to ¾ inch (1.3 to 2 cm) thick for an optimum ratio when sandwiched between the cookies. Cover the ice cream pans with tinfoil or plastic wrap and freeze them uncovered for 3 to 5 hours or overnight, until firm.

Begin making the cookies by preheating the oven to 350°F (177°C). Cream the butter in a standing mixer or with a hand mixer for about 30 seconds, and then add both of the sugars. Continue to cream until light and fluffy, about 30 seconds. Add the egg yolk. Mix until everything is well incorporated, and then add the baking soda. Give it another quick mix, and then add the dark cocoa powder and the flour. Mix until the dough is formed, about 30 seconds.

On a clean dry surface, dust a little flour and then roll out the cookie dough to ½ to ¾ inch (1.3 to 2 cm) thick. Using a 3- or 4-inch (8- or 10-cm) round or square biscuit or cookie cutter, cut out cookies in place on the baking sheet. Use a fork to gently poke some superficial holes in the top of the shortbread. Bake the cookies for 6 to 8 minutes, or until golden on the edges. Cool the cookies on the cookie sheet for 5 minutes, and then transfer them to a baking rack to cool completely. Place the cookies in the freezer for 1 hour for them to harden up. This will allow the cookie sandwiches to come together and stay frozen when assembling.

To make the sandwiches, it is best to work in batches so that both the ice cream and the cookies remain fully frozen. Remove six cookies and one pan of ice cream at a time. Using a 3- or 4-inch (8- or 10-cm) cookie or biscuit cutter, cut circles or squares into the ice cream and place each ice cream "disk" between two frozen cookies. Gently press down and refreeze the cookie sandwiches until you are ready to consume them. Repeat this process with the second pan of ice cream and the remaining six cookies. You may want to refreeze the ice cream for a short period of time if you find that it is becoming soft as you assemble the sandwiches.

Store any leftover cookies in a covered container in the freezer for up to 2 weeks.

OLD-FASHIONED CHOCOLATE CHIP COOKIE SANDWICHES

This recipe yields 12–14 ice cream cookie sandwiches.

There is nothing quite like vanilla ice cream sandwiched between two freshly baked chocolate chip cookies. It reminds me of my childhood, and the recreation of this old fashioned dessert is made simple and streamlined with no-churn ice cream and a classically wonderful chocolate chip cookie. You'll want to allow plenty of freeze time for this one if you want to enjoy firm ice cream sandwiches, but of course no one would blame you if you simply spooned the ice cream onto a warm cookie and enjoyed it just like that.

It is best to make the ice cream first, as it needs several hours (or overnight!) to become solid. Baking and freezing the cookies is step two, but by all means, reverse the steps if you'd like to enjoy some fresh baked cookies before or while you make the ice cream!

In a medium-sized bowl, make the ice cream by whisking together the sweetened condensed milk, pure vanilla extract and half-and-half until it is smooth. Set this aside. With a standing or hand mixer, whip the heavy cream until stiff peaks form, 60 to 90 seconds. Gently fold the sweetened condensed milk mixture into the cream that has been whipped. You will want this to be as smooth as possible and lump free.

Prepare two 8-inch (20-cm) round or square pans by lining them with parchment paper. Ensure that the parchment has a bit of overhang so that you can remove the ice cream as a whole unit once it is fully frozen.

Separate the ice cream into your two parchment-lined pans. Using a spatula, spread the ice cream evenly throughout the pans. You will want the ice cream to be ½ to ¾ inch (1.3 to 2 cm) thick for an optimum ratio when sandwiched between the cookies. Freeze the ice cream pans uncovered for 3 to 5 hours or overnight, until firm.

(continued)

For the Ice Cream

1 (14-oz [414-ml]) can sweetened condensed milk

1 tbsp (15 ml) pure vanilla extract

½ cup (120 ml) half-and-half

1½ cups (360 ml) heavy cream

1½ cup (255 g) semisweet chocolate chips

OLD-FASHIONED CHOCOLATE CHIP COOKIE SANDWICHES (CONT.)

For the Cookies

1 cup (228 g) salted butter, softened

¾ cup (165 g) firmly packed dark brown sugar

½ cup (100 g) granulated sugar

2 large eggs

1 tsp baking soda

1 tsp salt

2 tsp (10 ml) pure vanilla extract

2½ cups (320 g) all-purpose flour

2 cups (330 g) semi-sweet mini chocolate chips

VARIATION: *Substitute with the peanut butter ice cream from the Peanut Butter Party Cookie Sandwiches (page 131) and this is a whole new level of delicious.*

To make the cookies, begin by creaming the butter in a standing mixer or with a hand mixer for about 30 seconds, and then add both of the sugars. Continue to cream until light and fluffy, about 30 seconds. Add both eggs. Mix until well incorporated, and then add the baking soda, salt and pure vanilla extract. Give it another good mix, and then add the flour. Mix until dough is formed, about 30 seconds, and then add the mini chocolate chips. Stir gently until they are mixed in.

Preheat your oven to 375°F (190°C). Using a 2-teaspoon (10-ml) cookie scoop to make balls, spoon the balls onto a nonstick baking sheet and refrigerate for 1 hour. Remove the cookie dough from the refrigerator and bake for 11 to 12 minutes, or until the edges are golden. Cool the cookies on the cookie sheet for 5 minutes, and then transfer them to a baking rack to cool completely. Place the cookies in the freezer for 1 hour for them to harden up. This will allow the cookie sandwiches to come together and stay frozen when assembling.

To make the sandwiches, it is best to work in batches so that both the ice cream and the cookies remain fully frozen. Remove six cookies and one pan of ice cream at a time. Using a 3- or 4-inch (8- or 10-cm) cookie or biscuit cutter, cut circles into the ice cream and place each ice cream "disk" between two frozen cookies. Gently press down and refreeze the cookie sandwiches until you are ready to consume them. Repeat this process with the second pan of ice cream and the remaining six cookies. You may want to refreeze the ice cream for a short period of time if you find that it is becoming soft as you assemble the sandwiches.

Store any leftover cookies in a covered container in the freezer for up to 2 weeks.

COOKIE DOUGH ICE CREAM SANDWICHES

This recipe yields 12–14 ice cream cookie sandwiches.

This edible cookie dough ice cream sandwich creation is my absolute favorite chilled treat of all time. The cookie dough is eggless, so it is safe to eat. It boasts full cookie dough flavor with real vanilla, brown sugar and salted butter.

The edible cookie dough squares are frozen, then sandwiched around creamy vanilla bean ice cream. A drizzle of melted chocolate completes the decadence, and I promise that you will be going back for seconds, thirds and quite possibly even fourths!

It is best to make the cookie dough first, as it needs about an hour of refrigeration before it is solid enough to make the sandwiches. Making the ice cream is step two, but by all means, reverse the steps if you'd like to enjoy some tantalizing cookie dough before or while you make the ice cream!

In a small to medium-sized bowl, begin to make the cookie dough squares by creaming the butter and both sugars together with a wooden spoon, until smooth. Add in the heavy cream, pure vanilla extract and salt. Blend the mixture until everything is incorporated.

Add in the flour and mix well, finally folding the mini chocolate chips into the batter. Roll the edible cookie dough out between two sheets of parchment paper. You will want the cookie dough to be about ½ inch (1.3 cm) thick. Using a square cookie cutter (or round, that is fine too!), cut the cookie dough squares out and place them on a parchment-lined cookie sheet. Put the cookie sheet in the freezer for an hour to allow the cookie dough squares to harden.

(continued)

For the Edible Cookie Dough

½ cup (114 g) salted butter, softened

¼ cup (50 g) granulated sugar

½ cup (110 g) firmly packed brown sugar

2 tbsp (30 ml) heavy cream

1 tsp pure vanilla extract

½ tsp salt

1¼ cups (160 g) all-purpose flour*

¾ cup (124 g) mini chocolate chips

*It has been said that there is a small risk of E. coli when consuming raw flour. If this concerns you, microwave your flour for 1 minute 15 seconds, or until 160°F (71°C) temperature is reached. Allow the flour to cool completely and then proceed with the recipe.

COOKIE DOUGH ICE CREAM SANDWICHES (CONT.)

For the Ice Cream

1 (14-oz [414-ml]) can sweetened condensed milk

1 tbsp (15 ml) pure vanilla extract

½ cup (120 ml) half-and-half

1½ cups (360 ml) heavy cream

1 cup (165 g) semi-sweet chocolate chips

VARIATION: *You can pick any ice cream flavor in this book that you'd like to try with these edible cookie dough squares. I suggest the peanut butter ice cream from the Peanut Butter Party Cookie Sandwiches recipe (page 131), Rich Chocolate ice cream (page 13) or Bold Coffee ice cream (page 17).*

In a medium-sized bowl, make the ice cream by whisking together the sweetened condensed milk, pure vanilla extract and half-and-half, until the mixture is smooth. Set this aside. With a standing or hand mixer, whip the heavy cream until stiff peaks form, 60 to 90 seconds. Gently fold the sweetened condensed milk mixture into the cream that has been whipped. You will want this to be as smooth as possible and lump free.

Prepare two 8-inch (20-cm) round or square pans by lining them with parchment paper. Ensure that the parchment has a bit of overhang so that you can remove the ice cream as a whole unit once it is fully frozen.

Separate the ice cream into your two parchment-lined pans. Using a spatula, spread the ice cream evenly throughout the pans. You will want the ice cream to be ½ to ¾ inch (1.3 to 2 cm) thick for an optimum ratio when sandwiched between the cookies. Freeze the ice cream pans uncovered for 3 to 5 hours or overnight, until firm.

It is best to work in batches so that both the ice cream and the cookies remain fully frozen. Remove six cookies dough squares and one pan of ice cream at a time. Use the same cookie dough cutter that you used to cut out the cookie dough. Cut squares (or circles) of the ice cream and place each ice cream square between two frozen cookie dough pieces. Gently press down and refreeze the cookie sandwiches, until you are ready to consume them. Repeat this process with the second pan of ice cream and the remaining six cookies. You may want to refreeze the ice cream for a short period of time if you find that it is becoming soft as you assemble the sandwiches.

Melt the semi-sweet chocolate chips in a microwave-safe bowl for 60 seconds or until smooth. Keep heating for additional 30-second increments until the chocolate can be whisked smoothly. With a spoon or a piping bag, drizzle a little bit of chocolate onto about half the edible cookie sandwich. Repeat with each cookie sandwich. Refrigerate for 10 minutes and serve.

Store any leftover cookies in a covered container in the freezer for up to 2 weeks. Enjoy!

DIETARY SUBSTITUTIONS

I love providing gluten- and dairy-free substitutions so that those with alternate dietary needs can enjoy my recipes to their fullest! These are substitutions that I have used and continue to stock in my own home. I want your baking experience to be the best it can be, and avoiding gluten or dairy shouldn't hinder that process in the slightest.

Here is a list of tried-and-true dietary substitutes, so that you can enjoy these recipes without the additions of gluten or dairy. I have personally tried each of these substitutes and can attest to their quality and similarity in each of my recipes.

- Bob's Red Mill Gluten Free 1-to-1 Baking Flour is a wonderful all-purpose substitute for traditional flour, and it's cup for cup, so use the same measurements as you would all-purpose flour. The finished products come out slightly denser than with all-purpose flour, but the flavor and texture are quite similar.

- Miyoko's Butter is a plant-based brick that closely resembles dairy butter not only in its look, but its taste as well. It melts, browns and spreads just like real butter, and is truly a fantastic substitute. Use it as a one-to-one ratio substitute, the same as you would with the flour, so the recipe measurements will not change.

- Miyoko's also makes a wonderful cream cheese that works beautifully in my cheesecake ice cream recipes.

- Silk® Dairy-Free Heavy Cream and plant-based half-and-half are great options for replacing the dairy version in the base recipe for all of my ice creams.

- Sweetened condensed coconut milk can be used in all recipes to replace dairy condensed milk. Note that this product has a slight yet distinct coconut flavor that will be stronger in simpler recipes and more camouflaged in complex ones.

- Pamela's™ Honey Graham Crackers are gluten-free and perfect for use where graham crackers are called for.

ACKNOWLEDGMENTS

I owe everything to my beautiful Savior, Jesus Christ, for creating me, passionately pursuing my heart, holding every tear of mine in a bottle, celebrating every victory with me, and walking every step of this life beside me. You are my Father, my friend, my rock and my God. I would not be here without your amazing love and never-ending patience, and I will spend my life proclaiming your goodness with every breath that I have.

To my husband, Richard, my best friend, the one who makes me smile and laugh like no other, and who has encouraged this dream from the very start; I love you with my whole heart. Thanks for being the best taste tester ever, although you are not nearly picky enough and enjoy everything I make. I secretly love that about you, though. We have had many adventures together in this life we have built, and I can't wait for so many more.

To my precious sons, Conner, Bentley and Kingsley; words cannot express how blessed I am to be your mama. I thank the Lord every day for each of you individually, and I adore you three more than you will ever know. Thanks for being super picky tasters and loving Oreos more than my homemade cookies. It definitely keeps me grounded.

Mom and Dad, you are walking with Jesus in heaven right now and I miss you both so much, but I thank you for the amazing life you gave me. Thank you for baking together and showing me what love in the kitchen looked like. Thank you for letting me help, even when I knew it was more of a hindrance to the process! I can't wait to see you again one day, when we are reunited in Glory.

To my second parents, my incredible in-laws Randy and Lori; I struck gold with you both when I married your son. Thank you for loving me like a daughter and for believing in me. Your love and support means the world.

To Nick, Brittany, Kaelyn, Sandi, Malachi, Faith, Sydnie, Sandi N., Jennie, Tyler, Naomi and Natalie; siblings plus extended family as wonderful as all of you is definitely a rarity and I feel so blessed by each of you. I love you all.

To my amazing friends who eagerly enjoy my recipe tastings, to my husband's coworkers who give me way too much positive feedback because they are so lovely, to my former coworkers who joked about not letting me leave because the treats might end; I have loved sharing my process with you all. Thank you for letting me bounce recipes off you and thank you for the infinite kind words you have bestowed on me.

To the wonderful team at Page Street Publishing, there is no other way to say this except thank you for making my dream come true. I will never forget that first email asking if I wanted to pursue writing a book with you, and the day we made it official will always be one of the happiest professional moments in my career. From the bottom of my heart, thank you for all the hard work and dedication you gave to bringing this dream to life. I am forever grateful.

To my Heather's Home Bakery family, the ones who were there from the inception, and the ones who are newer to the crew, I appreciate EVERY SINGLE ONE OF YOU. Thank you for the comments, the likes, the saves, the shares, the blog visits, the reviews and everything else that has helped propel my baking hobby into a full-blown business. You are all rockstars, and I am so excited to keep journeying down this path with you.

ABOUT THE AUTHOR

Heather Templeton is the creator of Heather's Home Bakery, a sweets-focused blog that takes decadent desserts and brings them to life with step-by-step instructions and beautiful imagery. Heather's passion for baking began at a young age in the kitchen with her parents but didn't truly blossom until her oldest son was about to turn one. She wanted to make him a smash cake and baked her first-ever layer cake. She was hooked, and as the years progressed, went on to expand her offerings to include other goodies such as cookies, pies and, of course, ice cream.

Heather is a self-taught baker and food photographer who loves to share her recipes on her site. She loves Jesus, her husband and feels blessed beyond measure that she gets to be home with her three sons and build a life in beautiful Oregon.

INDEX